Common Sense about Common Core

Also by Jim Dueck

Being Fair with Kids
Education's Flashpoints

Common Sense about Common Core

Overcoming Education's Politics

Jim Dueck

ROWMAN & LITTLEFIELD
Lanham • Boulder • New York • London

Published by Rowman & Littlefield
A wholly owned subsidary of The Rowman & Littlefield Publishing Group, Inc.
4501 Forbes Boulevard, Suite 200, Lanham, Maryland 20706
www.rowman.com

Unit A, Whitacre Mews, 26-34 Stannary Street, London SE11 4AB

British Library Cataloguing in Publication Information Available

Library of Congress Cataloging-in-Publication Data

Names: Dueck, Jim, 1946– author.
Title: Common sense about Common Core : overcoming education's politics / by Jim Dueck.
Description: Lanham, Maryland : Rowman & Littlefield, 2016. | Includes bibliographical references and index.
Identifiers: LCCN 2015039403| ISBN 9781475823233 (cloth : alk. paper) | ISBN 9781475823240 (pbk. : alk. paper) | ISBN 9781475823257 (electronic)
Subjects: LCSH: Common Core State Standards (Education) | Education—Standards—United States—States.
Classification: LCC LB3060.83 .D84 2016 | DDC 379.1/58—dc23 LC record available at http://lccn.loc.gov/2015039403

∞ ™ The paper used in this publication meets the minimum requirements of American National Standard for Information Sciences Permanence of Paper for Printed Library Materials, ANSI/NISO Z39.48-1992.

Printed in the United States of America

Contents

Abbreviations

ACT—American College Testing
AFT—American Federation of Teachers
ARRA—American Recovery and Reinvestment Act
AYP—Adequate Yearly Progress
CBA—computer-based assessment
CCSS—Common Core State Standards
CCSSM—Common Core State Standards in Mathematics
CMEC—Council of Ministers of Education, Canada
ESEA—Elementary and Secondary Education Act
GPA—grade point average
LEAs—local educational agencies
NAEP—National Assessment of Educational Progress
NASH—National Association of System Heads
NCLB—No Child Left Behind
OECD—Organisation for Economic Co-operation and Development
PARCC—Partnership for Assessment of Readiness for College and Careers
PCAP—Pan-Canadian Assessment Program
PIRLS—Progress in International Reading Literacy Study
PISA—Programme for International Student Assessment
RttT—Race to the Top
SHEEO—State Higher Education Executive Officers Association
TIMSS—Trends in International Mathematics and Science Study
U.S. DoE—U.S. Department of Education

Preface

Forty years as an educator have made me acutely aware of the plethora of issues evident in accountability within the education system. Service in the classroom, principal's office, superintendent's chair, and educational leadership for a Canadian province as assistant deputy minister provided practical perspectives from all levels within the school system.

The Auditor General's Office for British Columbia identified me as the "most accountable superintendent" in the province, and the auditor general requested approval to have a team from his office interview stakeholders within the district. My program included providing financial incentives to schools for successfully improving student outcomes. Several suggestions for improving provincial outcomes were later implemented, including common assessments and reporting on school performance.

While providing leadership at the provincial level, school and district report cards were introduced featuring a combination of both raw (i.e., relative to fixed standards) and gain (i.e., relative to past performance) scores. This effort was one of the first to measure improvement and provide an evaluation based on multiple levels of performance. The success of this initiative resulted in approximately fifty delegations from around the world seeking to learn how educational accountability can work.

These delegations included Governor Tim Pawlenty, later a candidate for the U.S. presidency who wanted to learn about pay-for-performance in education; office staff from the United Kingdom's prime minister George Brown; and the minister of education from the United Kingdom, who subsequently requested a personal presentation on accountability in the House of Commons for his purpose of "infecting government bureaucrats."

Later, Linda Darling-Hammond, a well-known researcher in education and special consultant for Race to the Top, requested a presentation to aides in the White House, Congress, and the Governors' Association particularly focused on common assessment. This presentation was followed by a request from the Department of Education to assist in the launch of Race to the Top as well as sitting on the panel to identify pilots for common assessment. Out of these activities came invitations to identify winners of the various grants associated with the Race to the Top program.

In retirement, my role as a consultant has allowed time for helping candidates in civic politics, writing editorials for newspapers, and writing two books. The first book, *Being Fair with Kids*, provides the research base for helping parents understand that birth month is an important variable in student success. It concludes with a model for achieving 60 percent reduction in student failure and a minimum of 5 percent improvement in student achievement with a savings to a school district's budget of approximately 5 percent annually.

The second book, *Education's Flashpoints*, identifies many contentious issues in education and the impact these have had across several countries. The central problem identified is that teachers' unions exist to represent their members and not the students; therefore, this bias prevents the school system from being highly accountable and transparent. Politicians facilitate this ongoing flaw in the system because they covet teachers' votes and do little to inform the general population of the data surrounding many issues that would endanger support.

These experiences coupled with a lifetime of research provide the philosophical basis for this book. The central message endorses the U.S. governors' request for a Common Core supported by common assessment. No Child Left Behind was a watershed initiative in U.S. education because it provides additional funding when data indicates improvement in student outcomes. These additional funds are earned rather than being an entitlement. Race to the Top advances this form of accountability by introducing common assessment and incorporating performance into teacher pay. These principles are necessary components in transforming America's education system.

Introduction

The first section in this book deals with the motivation behind the request from governors across the U.S. for launching Common Core, and the myths and misunderstandings emerging as various special interests attempt to derail the initiative. Political motives are revealed, including those associated with capturing voter support in the 2016 presidential election. Each candidate's perspective is outlined within the context of why and how Common Core was initiated.

As the world becomes a global village, several factors are identified that now endanger the high level of trust that America's school system enjoyed for many decades. As trust wanes, it is no longer an entitlement enjoyed but an attitude earned. A new reality faces educators who must confront expectations for higher levels of accountability. One section outlines how No Child Left Behind, a bipartisan initiative under President George W. Bush, altered the distribution of education funding. Federal funding is relatively small compared with the total money spent in America's education system, but a requirement that these funds be earned was a shock to a system not used to focusing on performance.

A subsequent section then reveals how the school system is responding to the pressure for improved performance. On the one hand, states manipulated their tests so that more students demonstrate success. Teachers, too, manipulate success when they lower their standards by inflating the grades of their students. Whereas the manipulation at the state level was intentional, it is likely that the shift in the classroom was more subliminal, with a genuine desire to have students succeed. Regardless of the motivation, lack of consistency in interpreting student success is problematic because it produces unfair treatment for some students.

Rich data is presented, demonstrating the degree to which teachers' marks are inflated as well as how readily this occurs. It is significant that grade inflation is not uniformly evident across all student levels, which has implications regarding fairness to students, with some then being disadvantaged. Therefore, a section devoted to gender imbalance reveals how grade inflation benefits one gender more than the other. In other words, one gender experiences unfairness when teachers assess their classroom work.

Neutralizing grade inflation requires a coordinated effort across the participating states, and this book presents a need for common assessment. Simply, without common assessment, there is no assurance of Common Core. The absence of this principle in No Child Left Behind is its critical flaw, which Race to the Top attempts to rectify.

The next section deals with teachers' attitudes, which, while initially supportive of Common Core, now are shown to be skeptical of the initiative because common assessment permits comparison of performance. Race to the Top requires that student test scores become a component of teachers' evaluations and that these are then incorporated into the method for remunerating teachers. Moving away from paying teachers for their experience and certification to a method based on the outcome of their teaching is creating anxiety within the profession.

Common Core is necessary because it projects high standards on America's education system. The school system is in a rut of merely moving students through twelve years of schooling because of an ill-founded commitment to social promotion. Accountability for the academic success of each student is compromised. Therefore, a section is devoted to debunking myths associated with this practice.

While there are political hiccups in implementing Common Core, contrary to media reports, most states are moving forward. One section provides actual examples of how efforts to derail Race to the Top are addressed. Politics is messy, and the pathway to implementation requires many twists and turns. Some compromises defy logic.

Finally, the last chapter summarizes key points for achieving this transformational objective for reforming America's education system. Essentially, it means that students replace teachers atop the education pinnacle in order to ensure that fairness to all students occurs.

ONE

Americans Are Uninformed about Common Core

It is an understatement to suggest that American education is at a crossroads within current controversies regarding Common Core. It is equally an understatement that the current conceptualization in the political forum surrounding this concept is misrepresenting the facts to a public ill prepared to understand the many nuances involved. The politicization currently underway is riddled with *inaccurate statements and superficial debate* regarding an initiative designed to achieve greater levels of fairness for all American students.

Fairness for all students must be a significant goal within any debate regarding quality of education. When the evidence demonstrates that students are deprived of opportunity because their educational experiences are below standard, the system is failing the government that funds it, the parents who have lofty aspirations for their offspring, and the students who are prevented from achieving their potential.

Too many students have been penalized and disadvantaged for too many decades in an education system in a country that, at one time, may have been a world leader. What may have been is definitely not what presently exists. The problem is exacerbated by statements of good intentions but with limited progress evident due to political interference from both ends of the political spectrum. Unfortunately, political haranguing continues to confuse the public (specifically, parents), and it disadvantages too many students.

EDUCATION IS FAILING EXPECTATIONS

Periodically, governments release reports regarding the state of their education system to stimulate reform. In the United States, the 1983 release of the report *A Nation at Risk* was a landmark event that unsettled the educational system. In memorable language, it stated, *"If an unfriendly foreign power had attempted to impose on America the mediocre educational performance that exists today, we might well have viewed it as an act of war."* Such a graphic description of failure left an unsuspecting citizenry and vested interest groups incensed, and many subsequent statements sought to reassure the public that all was well.

Yet American students' performance on international tests such as the Trends in International Mathematics and Science Study (TIMSS), Progress in International Reading Literacy Study (PIRLS), and Programme for International Student Assessment (PISA) clearly demonstrated that the United States was at risk. The low levels of achievement on these assessments provided ample evidence for introducing reforming federal initiatives such as President Bush's No Child Left Behind (NCLB) and President Obama's Race to the Top (RttT). *Such a high level of presidential interest in education is a relatively recent phenomenon.*

Pearson, the publishing company, now combines results from international tests on cognitive skills with educational attainment in literacy and graduation rates. Its "Learning Curve" provides a global ranking of education systems for forty OECD (Organisation for Economic Co-operation and Development) countries, which further underscores the relative poor performance by the United States. Americans have a sense of pride in achieving high levels of performance, which is not consistent with what is evident in educational outcomes.

In Pearson's 2012 edition of global rankings, the United States had an overall ranking of seventeenth out of forty countries. By 2014, the U.S. ranking improved to fourteenth as a result of recent successes in cognitive skills—achieved through No Child Left Behind—with an eleventh place ranking. In the Educational Attainment index, the United States ranked twentieth overall. If such an American ranking occurred in the Olympics, for example, the media would portray the results as catastrophic. Yet, in education, mainline media is relatively low key about low levels of performance, likely because they do not wish to offend the sizeable workforce in education.

Pearson's methodology provides another version of assessing education systems around the world. Regardless of the system used, the evidence suggests that the United States is well down the ladder on key performance measures of student achievement. Pursuing another national attempt at educational reform is necessary in order to *ensure that all children receive fair treatment* by participating in educational programs with high standards.

In this pursuit, however, *the focus must change from trotting out another program that requires significant expense.* Rather, there must be an effort in which expectations for schools are increased through acknowledging that if high levels of student achievement are occurring somewhere, they should occur everywhere. *Political activity that is focused on ensuring that all students have access to high-quality service and outcomes is now a necessity. Continuing to operate as little fiefdoms without a coordinated strategy, while participating in a global community, is outlandish and outdated.*

Indeed, in preliminary discussion leading to the 2016 presidential election, debate over a coordinated strategy, known as *Common Core*, inexplicably is a major focus within both the Democratic and the Republican parties. Yet the media is focused on military conflicts in the Middle East and Russian incursion into Ukraine. There is racial tension because of police shootings of unarmed black men. Media analysts are preoccupied with the political maneuvering behind government shutdowns because of budgetary wrangling. There remains a persistent attack against the Affordable Care Act (also known as Obamacare). Media reporting on the effects of bad weather occurs almost nightly.

INATTENTIVE MEDIA IS PROBLEMATIC

The media delves into these issues with considerable detail doing whatever is necessary to bring actual film into their report. Their vigor and rigor is commendable because considerable personal risk is evident when reporting on many of the aforementioned issues. Within a few brief moments, citizens are "brought up to speed" with knowledge sufficient to carry on a reasonable conversation the next day.

Inexplicably, the media does little to unveil the complex issues in education such as the introduction of the Common Core. Perhaps their silence indicates tacit agreement with Jonathon Gruber's contentious statement about the public's capacity to understand complex issues. Gruber, a government administration adviser who assisted in crafting the Affordable Care Act, was roundly criticized when he was caught explaining the political deception involved within Obamacare while taxing so-called Cadillac insurance plans.

In a lecture at Washington University in St. Louis in October 2013 Gruber made an infamous comment recorded on tape to the effect that *"the American voter is too stupid to understand."* His response to the furor subsequently reported in the media was that the remark was "inappropriate." Perhaps it was, but some conditions prompted him to make such a remark, and we cannot merely dismiss a well-known saying that *many a true word is spoken in jest.* Was Gruber merely jesting or musing?

Revisiting this moment is not an attempt to vilify or defend Gruber; rather, the intention is to challenge the media to invest more time in understanding and then reporting on issues not easily covered within a fifteen second sound-bite or a short video. People live busy lives and they look to the media to provide information about important happenings in their world.

Klein (2014) refers to a similar situation with Common Core that may be related to Gruber's thoughts regarding Obamacare. She avoids any reference regarding people's capacity to understand and explains that "a major change is coming to a majority of public schools throughout the country, and most Americans have no idea what it is." In other words, *Americans are not being adequately informed.* The media is failing to provide citizens with information necessary to participate in discussions regarding a significant issue that will influence the country's future well-being.

Klein bases her conclusion on a survey conducted in 2014 that utilized interviews with 6,400 registered voters across the country. It found that:

- 31 percent support the standards
- 12 percent oppose the standards
- *58 percent have no knowledge of the standards*
- survey results were relatively consistent from region to region across the country

Common Core, a term that is already more than five years old, *represents a significant transformational change in American education;* yet the majority of the American public is oblivious to its content and intent.

Student achievement varies substantially across the United States, and standardized test results demonstrate that these variances in student achievement levels are not being ameliorated. There appears to be acceptance that some areas of the nation will provide children with good education and others will not. Hence, it is notable that a follow-up question in the survey indicated that two out of three (66 percent) of Americans "strongly supported uniform standards." Confusion within the public stems from substituting "standards" with the word "core." *Correct terminology may have assuaged much of the criticism and confusion surrounding Common Core.*

Achieve, an educational organization also active in polling, reported survey results on its website in 2015 and "found that while both the public and educators strongly support the notion of all states having common standards, there is low awareness, especially among the general voting public, of the Common Core State Standards (CCSS)." For example, "only 19 percent of voters have seen, read and/or heard anything about the Common Core." This report concludes that "when more details on the CCSS are given, support rises significantly."

The report also determined, "Public education is considered to be a very or extremely important issue to voters across the board. However, only about one in ten voters—including educators—believe public education is working pretty well right now." Therefore, another finding in the report provides a glimpse into where *opposition to aspects of Common Core* may emerge. Specifically,

> The general public strongly supports using the results for a full range of accountability purposes, while teachers are more skeptical of using test results for such purposes. For example, at least three-quarters of voters said it was acceptable to use test data for holding districts, schools or teachers accountable. Among teachers, a slim majority (51 percent) believe it is acceptable to use test results to hold districts and schools accountable, but only 39 percent believe this data should be used for teacher accountability.

The degree to which this issue is controversial and has potential to create confusion will be discussed later.

BOMBASTIC COMMENTARY

While public support for uniform standards across the nation received strong support, some individuals are contributing a decidedly negative perspective: Klein (2014) documented several strongly worded dissenting opinions:

- "What the heck am I talking about? The end of the world? Some kind of natural disaster? Zombies? No, something even scarier: the Common Core." (David Kierski)
- "Most of us who lived through this Hitler era remember how British Prime Minister Chamberlain gushed how great Hitler's Youth Corps was, much like those who support Common Core today." (Donald Conkey, *Cherokee Tribune*)
- "This is the progressive movement coming in for the kill. And believe me, if we don't stop it, this will be the kill." (Glenn Beck)
- "Allowing the federal government at the throats of our young people is to disallow children the opportunity to know the unique American experience of liberty in a freewill republic." (Jim Mullen)
- "Remember the quote by Hitler, 'Give me your children and in 10 years I'll change society'? The Obama administration intends to do just that." (Elois Zeanah)
- "ObamaCore is a comprehensive plan to dumbdown schoolchildren so they will be the obedient servants of the government and probably to indoctrinate them to accept the leftwing view of America and its history." (Phyllis Schafly)
- "It [Common Core] sends shivers down the spines of freedom loving individuals." (Common Constitutionalist, Political Outcast)
- "Now they're teaching something called Common Core. Folks, this president is emulating dictators." (Bradlee Dean)
- If this isn't Nazism, Communism, Marxism and all the 'ism's' I don't know what it is." (Christina Michas)

Dissent is healthy in making good decisions especially when it is informed dissent. These strongly worded statements are intended to generate fear and distrust in the direction proposed for American education. *They evoke horrific images from the past and are likely intended to scare people from even undertaking an in-depth discovery of Common Core.* While these may be examples of more extreme reactions, the political calendar is conducive to generating significant controversy because a new concept is under consideration. *Indeed, it is conceivable that the 2016 presidential election will be significantly influenced by a candidate's perspective on Common Core.*

Fearmongering, a tactic frequently used to dissuade potential supporters, occurs whenever a new initiative is proposed. Common Core contained a commitment to have common standards that will raise levels of learning for all states. Schmidt (2012) studied the new standards for mathematics and endeavors to allay fear within the public arena by his analysis:

> The new Common Core State Standards in Mathematics (CCSSM) represent a major change in the way U.S. schools teach mathematics. Rather than a fragmented system in which content is "a mile wide and an inch deep," the new common standards offer the kind of mathematics instruction we see in the top-achieving nations, where students learn to master a few topics each year before moving on to more advanced mathematics. Together with my colleague Richard Houang, I've done some research looking at the CCSSM to see if it can improve student achievement. . . . We found that the new standards closely resemble the standards of those countries that do best in mathematics. The CCSSM demonstrates three key characteristics of a strong curriculum: they are focused (in that they concentrate on a few topics every year), rigorous (with grade-level appropriate material), and coherent (move from simpler to more sophisticated topics). We also found that those states whose old standards were more like the CCSSM did better on the National Assessment of Educational Progress (NAEP), the gold standard for U.S. national assessments.

This book is about unravelling the confusion surrounding Common Core and demonstrating why common standards are necessary for the United States' future well-being. Success in learning is related to enhanced quality of life for citizens, and it is time to change course from a system that is disadvantaging too many students. *Indeed, the current education system is unfair to many of America's children.* Supporting a system devoid of common standards is deleterious to the nation's future role within the global community.

Lack of accurate information from the media is contributing to a proliferation of many myths designed to discredit the Common Core initiative. Rather than debating merit from a knowledgeable perspective, many Americans, including politicians, are being *swept into ideological camps based on innuendo, "myth-information," and deceit.* Assisting citizens to become knowledgeable requires a more active role by the media so that they can lay out the issues for greater public understanding. This role is essential in a democracy and, at this point in time, *Americans are being failed.*

The key points made in this chapter are as follows:

- Too many students have been penalized and disadvantaged for too many decades in an education system in a country that, at one time, may have been a world leader.
- America's rankings on international assessments of student learning are consistently below expectations.
- Common Core is a significant educational initiative, but its importance is not evident to the American public because of mass media inattention.
- A lack of understanding about Common Core contributes to unrealistic rhetoric and fear-mongering from some reactionaries in the media.
- The media is failing the public by not bringing clarity to a complex educational issue.

TWO

The Myth of Federal Government Overreach

Discussions with the public regarding Common Core frequently focus on the notion that this initiative is an example of federal government overreach. Government's increasing size and involvement in people's lives is a partisan issue in American politics, especially with members of the Republican Party who are more inclined toward smaller and less intrusive government. Therefore, anything construed to be overreach with an education initiative of this magnitude readily becomes a national election issue for those seeking political office.

EDUCATION IS THE PURVIEW OF THE STATE

Contextually speaking, education is the purview of the state. The Tenth Amendment of the U.S. Constitution states, "The powers not delegated to the United States by the Constitution, nor prohibited by it to the States, are reserved to the States respectively, or to the people." The absence of references to education in the Constitution therefore *reserves authority over educational matters to the states.*

Lurie (2013) perceives the absence of constitutional authority for the federal government as a significant weakness in American politics. His analysis of constitutions worldwide is that 174—almost every country other than the United States—provide for a "constitutional guarantee to education." Omitting references to education appears to then *promote territorialism among the states* whereby any pursuit of "common" requires

11

negotiation and consent. *Efforts to reform are splintered, which may not be in the best interests of the entire country.* Nevertheless, it is what it is, and American education is within a state's mandate.

Opposition to current perceptions of overreach by the U.S. Department of Education is so great a concern to the right-wing element within the Republican Party that in February 2015, an attempt by lawmakers to amend the No Child Left Behind legislation was withdrawn because of resistance from conservatives. Harkness (2015) reported on the withdrawn amendments in the Republican-controlled House:

> After failing to win the support of conservatives, Republicans have quietly withdrawn legislation that would update the No Child Left Behind law by scaling back Washington's involvement in education. The bill, called the Student Success Act, was strongly opposed by both conservatives and Democrats.
>
> "Conservatives across the country had voiced concerns that the policy contained in this 620-page rewrite of [No Child Left Behind] did not limit Washington's overreach into education," said Lindsey Burke, The Heritage Foundation's Will Skillman Fellow in Education. *Their voices, expressing concern that this proposal represents a missed opportunity to restore state and local control of education and empower parents, have been heard.*
>
> Conservatives opposed the Student Success Act because they feel it did not go far enough in reducing the federal government's imprint in state and local education policy. Democrats argued it went too far.

While there are many myths evident in the debate regarding Common Core, none is more crucial to understanding this issue than is the debate concerning overreach. In simplest terms, Common Core *did not originate with the federal government's Department of Education;* rather, it originated with the states, specifically the governors. It is a proposal by an overwhelming majority of the states to create clear, consistent standards. Direction in this proposal *originated with state governors and not from a federal body.* It is intended to raise standards in student achievement in all participating states.

Camera (2015) reviewed nation-wide polls regarding the public's sentiment toward Common Core, and concluded, "While awareness of the standards jumped in the past year, many U.S. adults have misperceptions that the standards are a federal initiative: support for the standards by teachers is slipping; and there is a steep partisan divide over the common core." The observation regarding teachers' support will be the subject of another chapter in this book; however, additional comment regarding the public's perception is warranted.

These polls demonstrate that much of the blame for public opposition is based on the belief that Common Core is a federal initiative. Camera reports on an interview with the CEO of the PDK/Gallup poll, William Bushaw, who suggests that "the unfulfilled promise lawmakers made that NCLB would result in all students being proficient by this year has left a bad taste in many people's mouths." He says further:

> I think we missed how the [No Child Left Behind Act] legislation is impacting Americans' opinions about public school and about the federal role. I argue that's part of the equation with the common core. Unfortunately, it looks like a federal initiative when it's not, and Americans are skeptical right now of the federal role given what's happened with NCLB.

Camera's review also concluded:

> Of those who opposed the common core in the PDK/Gallup poll, 40 percent said that one of the most important reasons was their belief that the federal government initiated the standards, and 38 percent cited their view that the common core will result in a national curriculum and national tests.

In addition to this misunderstanding regarding Common Core's origin, is the confusion associated with the branding used for the initiative. One poll—Education Next—explored whether the words "Common Core" produced opposition from the public more than when the brand is changed to *common standards*. The poll asked a follow-up question on whether respondents support or oppose the use of the Common Core standards, but it replaced "Common Core" with the phrase "standards for reading and math that are the same across the states." When the label was dropped from the question, support for the Common Core increased to 68 percent from 53 percent.

Words are important and the Common Core initiative is plagued by a communications issue where many in the public acquired a different meaning than what is factual. This unfortunate error resulted in a sizeable percentage of the population believing that Common Core was a federal initiative determining what is taught in the nation's public schools. *This misinterpretation is now producing an election issue dominated by partisan politics.*

The *Education Next* poll found that the majorities of both Republicans and Democrats supported the common-core standards in 2013, but that support among Republicans fell in 2014 from 57 percent to 43 percent. Support among Democrats remained nearly unchanged, with 64 percent in favor in 2013 and 63 percent in 2014. Common Core is an initiative launched by governors during a Democratic presidency, and this drop in Republican support should not be surprising. In a polarized political environment, one of the parties will almost always oppose what has occurred during the other party's term in power.

Leading up to the 2016 elections, "ObamaCare" and "ObamaCore" are two terms sometimes used by politicians and recorded in the media. The former was a health initiative at the direction of President Obama while the latter is not, but is an education initiative sponsored by a consortium of state governors during President Obama's term in office. The one-letter change is clever politics intended to link two entirely separate issues, thereby inflaming political partisanship. *While this may be a clever substitution, it is also premeditated deceit.*

STATE GOVERNORS' MOTIVATION FOR COMMON CORE

Common Core is not an initiative of the U.S. Department of Education. Governors recognized that many students across the nation are treated unfairly because educational standards are so disparate. Students graduating from school in one state do not have the same level of skills and knowledge as students from other states, and these disparities remain substantial. Displaying the evidence that governors used to mobilize the Common Core initiative provides additional understanding of why they assumed this leadership role.

The data found in table 2.1 records the percentage of fifteen-year-old students for each state who wrote the 2012 PISA international tests in mathematics and reading, and who scored at the "proficient" level. The disparity in student success between Massachusetts and Mississippi, for example, clearly demonstrates the substantial difference that students have in their preparation for high school, and ultimately college and university.

The differences between state results demonstrate how unfair it is for students being educated in a state where schools provide inferior education. It is important that these variances be ameliorated because *students*

Table 2.1.

Math	(% Proficient)	Reading	(% Proficient)
Massachusetts	50.7	Massachusetts	43.0
Minnesota	43.1	Vermont	42.1
Vermont	41.4	New Jersey	39.0
North Dakota	41.0	Montana	38.9
New Jersey	40.4	New Hampshire	37.2
Kansas	40.2	Connecticut	37.1
South Dakota	39.1	Maine	36.9
Pennsylvania	38.3	South Dakota	36.8
New Hampshire	37.9	Minnesota	36.6
Montana	37.6	Pennsylvania	36.4
Virginia	37.5	Ohio	35.9
Colorado	37.4	Iowa	35.7
Wisconsin	37.0	Kansas	35.2
Maryland	36.5	Nebraska	35.2
Wyoming	36.0	Colorado	34.6
Washington	35.9	Washington	34.1
Ohio	35.4	Oregon	34.0
Iowa	35.2	Virginia	33.7
Indiana	35.1	Wisconsin	33.2
Oregon	34.8	Wyoming	33.2
Connecticut	34.7	Maryland	33.2
Texas	34.7	New York	33.2
Nebraska	34.6	North Dakota	33.2
North Carolina	34.5	Idaho	31.6
Maine	34.1	**United States**	**31.2**
Idaho	34.1	Indiana	31.1
Utah	32.4	Missouri	31.0
Alaska	32.4	Delaware	30.5
United States	**32.4**	Utah	30.1
South Carolina	31.9	Illinois	29.8
Delaware	31.3	Michigan	28.2
Illinois	30.8	Florida	28.0
New York	30.2	North Carolina	28.0
Missouri	29.9	Kentucky	27.7

Michigan	28.9	Texas	27.5
Rhode Island	27.7	Rhode Island	27.2
Florida	27.4	Alaska	27.1
Kentucky	27.3	Oklahoma	26.1
Arizona	26.3	Georgia	25.6
Georgia	24.7	Tennessee	25.6
Arkansas	24.4	Arkansas	25.4
California	23.9	South Carolina	24.6
Tennessee	23.1	Arizona	24.3
Nevada	23.0	West Virginia	22.9
Oklahoma	21.3	Nevada	21.5
Hawaii	21.2	California	21.5
Louisiana	19.0	Alabama	21.2
West Virginia	18.5	Hawaii	20.3
Alabama	18.2	Louisiana	19.4
New Mexico	17.4	Mississippi	17.4
Mississippi	13.6	New Mexico	17.3
District of Columbia	8.0	District of Columbia	12.1

proceed through the school system only once and governments must ensure that all students are recipients of a quality learning experience characterized by high standards.

In another review of educational performance, Merrefield (2011) examined results of student achievement in grades 4 and 8 in the National Assessment of Educational Progress (NAEP). This comparison focused on two states—Massachusetts and Mississippi—in order to demonstrate the degree to which students in Mississippi are disadvantaged educationally.

Massachusetts

Fourth-grade students at or above the advanced level, Math: *12 percent*
Number of states that performed better, at a statistically significant level: *0*
Eighth-grade students at or above the advanced level, Math: *17 percent*
Number of states that performed better, at a statistically significant level: *0*

Fourth-grade students at or above the advanced level, Reading: *13 percent*

Number of states that performed better, at a statistically significant level: *0*

Eighth-grade students at or above the advanced level, Reading: *5 percent*

Number of states that performed better, at a statistically significant level: *0*

Average number of states that performed better than Massachusetts, per test: *0*

Mississippi

Fourth-grade students at or above the advanced level, Math: *2 percent*

Number of states that performed better, at a statistically significant level: *47*

Eighth-grade students at or above the advanced level, Math: *2 percent*

Number of states that performed better, at a statistically significant level: *48*

Fourth-grade students at or above the advanced level, Reading: *4 percent*

Number of states that performed better, at a statistically significant level: *35*

Eighth-grade students at or above the advanced level, Reading: *1 percent*

Number of states that performed better, at a statistically significant level: *46*

Average number of states that performed better than Mississippi, per test: *44*

Any debate regarding Common Core must include discussion regarding the lack of fairness for students evident in this comparison. While Merrefield's comparison focused on two states that demonstrate the greatest variance, multiple other comparisons would also result in a conclusion that *the variance is unacceptable*—just not to the same degree. In the PISA chart, for example, is it a concern that Rhode Island had 27.7 percent of its students achieve at the "proficient" level in math, while Massachusetts had 50.7 percent?

When we examine student achievement across all states, it is only logical that parents, in particular, and voters, in general, wonder how acceptable it is to see substantial variations in students' test scores. What is the acceptable degree of tolerance before parents sound the alarm indicating that their child will leave their schooling with an inferior education? An unfair educational situation for segments of the nation's youth is evident; yet *too many politicians are pursuing power and control.*

No Child Left Behind, an initiative under Republican president Bush, was an attempt to lever school improvement. Additional funding to further improve student achievement was available when schools met improvement targets. Expecting schools to improve levels of student achievement made sense, and the public's concern with American schools was sufficient to tolerate federal government involvement. NCLB's initial support from both Republicans and Democrats (particularly Senator Edward Kennedy) provided evidence that the parties were working "across the aisle." *Federal government overreach into education at that time appeared to be acceptable.*

Unfortunately, NCLB had a major weakness. By exposing dramatic disparities in student achievement across states and schools, it demonstrated how human nature can respond to pressure when accountability is introduced. When there is a program to reward improvement, politicians and administrators want their organizations to qualify. Leadership within organizations will be confronted when improvement does not occur, especially when there is success evident elsewhere; however, consequences must be applied to politicians when they intentionally game the system to the detriment of their students.

NCLB outlined a process for rewarding leadership but failed to provide a consistent standard for *measuring leadership's* success. Rather than impose a standardized measurement tool, such as is available with NAEP, *it left measurement up to each state.* Without applying a consistent standard, individual states manipulated downward the difficulty of their assessments in order that schools might qualify in meeting their improvement targets. *In simple terms, the federal government was defrauded by political forces within many states to persuade their taxpayers that schools were performing to expectations.*

Figure 2.1 documents the 2009 grade 4 NAEP reading results by state, which demonstrates the fraudulent behavior and the need for Common Core. This study by the U.S. Department of Education indicated how states manipulated their own tests to qualify for annual NCLB improvement grants. By 2009, all states' grade 4 reading tests demonstrated that their "proficient standard" was below America's national testing program equivalent. More reprehensible, most states' "proficiency" level is actually below NAEP's "basic." States could have selected NAEP as their measurement tool; however, they would have lost *the ability to manipulate* the standards on their tests.

The point in drawing attention to these dramatic variations is to underscore why governors directed development of Common Core. Certainly some governors would have felt embarrassed by seeing how students in their states performed relative to others. *Politicians must accept accountability for the outcomes of their leadership and deal with the pressure to ensure that the unfair situation is turned around.* All leadership makes a difference, although sometimes the difference is *negative rather than positive.*

At the same time, there was no opportunity for those governors of high-performing states to feel proud when, among the thirty-four OECD countries, the United States performed below average in mathematics in 2012 and was ranked in twenty-seventh place (this is the best estimate,

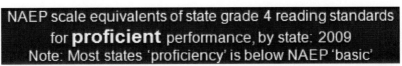

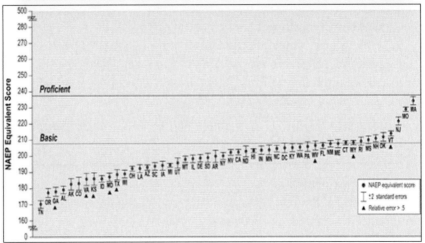

Figure 2.1.

although the rank could be between twenty-three and twenty-nine due to sampling and measurement error). Performance in both reading and science is close to the OECD average. The United States ranks seventeenth in reading (range of ranks: 14–20) and twentieth in science (range of ranks: 17–25). Notably, there has been no significant change in these performances over time.

There can be no equivocating by any politicians and their supporters who claim that Common Core is overreach by the U.S. Department of Education. Governors had already triggered the initiative to develop consistent standards prior to the American Recovery and Reinvestment Act, which then provided the federal government's Race to the Top grant program. These standards were approved by individual states without involvement of the U.S. Congress. *Those who belabor the overreach concept have some other purpose in mind.*

Governors—or at least the forty-five who wanted their states to participate in RttT—later reiterated their commitment to the Common Core concept when they submitted their application to participate in pilot assessment programs under RttT. As a member of the review committee, we confirmed that each application contained the governor's signature, as well as the signature of each education secretary and every college and university president within the state.

The signatures of the post-secondary institutions were important because they committed to:

1. accepting the schools' marks based on RttT assessments as the students' final mark, and
2. canceling all remediation classes in their institutions because these types of programs are no longer necessary when the students' marks applying to institutions are also based on graduation requirements specified in the Common Core.

Government was basically *paying double for too many students entering post-secondary programs.* Taxpayers were footing the bill when students were in grades 11 and 12 and then, again, when these ill-prepared students required remediation upon entry to college. Common Core is intended to ensure that students passing grade 12 can demonstrate a standard necessary for college and career readiness.

Finally, proponents of the overreach theory need to reconsider their position in view of the *optional nature* states have in adopting Common

Core. Nationally, forty-five states and the District of Columbia originally adopted the standards between 2010 and 2011. There were five states—Texas, Alaska, Minnesota, Virginia, and Nebraska—which chose to remain outside of the fold, providing additional evidence that *participation is within the control of each state.* Ohio also exercised its local control in this matter by repealing its earlier decision to participate.

In summary, a strong case could be made that overreach by the U.S. Department of Education (US DoE) is necessary. In virtually all countries, the national government is involved in educational matters. Data demonstrates wide variations in student achievement across the states, and the United States is certainly not regarded as an educational powerhouse based on international assessments.

There is a degree of irony evident in this discussion regarding federal government overreach. NCLB is one program that is already managed by the US DoE, and it was sponsored by a Republican president with strong support from both parties in Congress. There is no justification for accusations, however, that development of Common Core is the result of the US DoE overstepping its mandate. This initiative is at the request and direction of the governors and their states that elected to participate. The simple fact that some states chose not to join the Common Core initiative demonstrates that involvement is a local decision.

The key points made in this chapter are as follows:

- Education is a state responsibility.
- Common Core is not federal government overreach because it originated with state governors.
- Common Core is plagued by a communications issue where many in the public acquired a different meaning than what is factual.
- Many students across the nation were being treated unfairly because educational standards across the states are so disparate.
- No Child Left Behind, a federal government initiative, is an example where overreach into education appeared to be acceptable to both political parties.
- NCLB was plagued by not requiring common assessment to prevent states from reducing the difficulty of their tests.
- Proponents of the overreach theory need to reconsider their position in view of the *optional nature* states have in adopting and remaining within Common Core.

THREE

Standards versus Curriculum

All careers are plagued with code words that create confusion for people not directly involved with a specific type of work. In baseball, for example, a "walk-off home run" is a significant event because it is directly focused on the home team and, therefore, most of the fans in the ballpark. It is not only a home run but also a climactic event that abruptly ends a baseball game in favor of the home team. Ensuing jubilation about this event produces great fanfare as the hitter rounds the bases and then literally jumps on home plate, while being mobbed by teammates. The event culminates with everyone—players and umpires—walking off the field: game over!

People not knowledgeable about baseball would be mystified by hearing the term, walk-off home run. Their lack of understanding makes them gullible to many far-fetched explanations. Baseball has many terms requiring deeper understanding of the game, and this is a fact of life in all aspects of human endeavor. Nuances may appear trivial, but, for those associated with an area of work, *the precise meaning of terminology is important.*

In education, there is jargon that can confuse parents and the public to such an extent that many arrive at erroneous conclusions. It is evident in communications with non-educators, for when they hear the term *Common Core,* they often confuse it as being synonymous with the word *curriculum.* This confusion is producing misleading rhetoric for the 2016 presidential election as candidates seek to exploit opponents' positions

on an issue that separates the various contenders into different philosophical camps.

COMMON CORE VERSUS CURRICULUM

In 2009, during a meeting involving a team of international education
experts with White House and congressional aides as well as the Governors' Council, Roy Romer explained a thoughtful conclusion made by
governors across the United States. Romer, a long-serving political figure,
was the superintendent of Los Angeles Unified School District, three-
term governor of Colorado, chair of the Democratic Governors' Association, and chairman of the Education Commission of the States. At the
time of this meeting he served as chairman and lead spokesman for the
nonprofit project, Strong American Schools.

These varied and extensive roles provided Romer with insight into the
politics of education: notably where does the field of education lie within
the context of the U.S. Constitution? Chapter 2 reminds readers that "the
powers not delegated to the United States by the Constitution, nor prohibited by it to the States, are reserved to the States respectively, or to the
people." The absence of references to education in the Constitution therefore reserves authority over educational matters to the states.

School curriculum is *not* conceptualized within the Constitution, and
Romer informed the international team that the Governors' Association
was working to reform education throughout the United States by carefully avoiding the word curriculum. The Fulbright Commission website,
which analyzes differences between U.S. and UK school systems, summarizes the U.S. governance model in education as follows:

> Authority over public (state-funded) school education in the US rests
> primarily with individual state departments of education. As most pol-
> icies are set at the state and local levels, the school curriculum can vary
> from state to state and even between school districts within a state.
> Therefore [the] best point of contact will usually be the local school or
> school board.

Some blurring in responsibilities for curriculum between the state and
school district may exist, but this area is completely off limits to the
federal government's Department of Education. This federal department's mandate is to ensure that all states have challenging and clear

standards of achievement and accountability for all children, not to mention effective strategies for reaching those standards.

In other words, *curriculum content is the discretion of the state and local school boards.* They choose what will be taught as well as the resources that will be used to support teachers in the classroom. Not only is the content outside the purview of the federal government, but the strategies employed by teachers in teaching the curriculum are also determined by the teacher and their school districts, who are responsible for managing their workforce. Teachers may receive support from their unions, teacher training institutions and colleagues regarding how to facilitate student learning.

In his comments with the international team, Romer believed it necessary to assist our understanding that the federal government was not meddling in education, which could eventually undo the reform effort through a successful court challenge. The reform's emphasis was on *standards*, which articulate whether the student has performed well or poorly on a given task. *These standards articulated in the Common Core are approved by each participating state, and states have flexibility to opt out at any time. These provisions are frequently overlooked by people in the public arena who wish to create controversy for nefarious purposes.*

AMERICANS ARE CONFUSED WITH COMMON CORE

Many Americans struggle with understanding the term Common Core and how it will impact classrooms. The annual PDK/Gallup poll for 2014 reported that 60 percent of Americans opposed having teachers in their community use the Common Core State Standards to guide what they teach, while only 33 percent were in favor. Discussions with parents frequently reveal their misunderstanding that CCSS is a curriculum: a belief buttressed by an inability for individual states to make changes to the Common Core.

There is a lack of understanding within the public that *Common Core is developed by a consortium of states* and, therefore, that some control at the individual state level is lost *voluntarily.* This is not unlike what occurred decades ago as individual school boards yielded absolute control over curriculum when embracing a state's curriculum. This transferring of control to a larger entity occurred more than a century earlier when the curriculum was controlled by the school and, perhaps, even within individual classrooms. *What occurred within a classroom once the door was closed was so private that the teacher was the sole determinant of what happened, including what was taught.*

As the population urbanized and regions became more densely populated, school districts assumed greater coordination of curriculum. Although teachers received little detail on what to teach, documents now contained more specific information about topics and concepts that must be taught as well as learning outcomes that students must achieve. As the pace of travel and communications increased and communities were no longer so isolated, the ability of state governments to monitor what was occurring in its schools improved.

Now that we are in a global village, it is not surprising that states are banding together to pursue a common set of standards, which is not only cost effective but also a means for ratcheting up expectations for their respective state. States evaluate student outcomes of their curricula relative to that of other states and determine whether expectations are sufficiently challenging within their purview. The capacity to make comparisons is perceived as a threat by many within the education system because they can be and are being held accountable for results. This conflict is discussed in more detail later.

A key point in this discussion remains the fact that individual states and their school districts can *adopt any curriculum while paying heed to Common Core standards.* Their assessment is not necessarily based on the curriculum used in classrooms, albeit state-level administrators are wise to align their curriculum with the assessments. Assessments of student learning are based on the Common Core standards deemed necessary for an educated citizen in the United States.

Similarly, there is no stipulation on resources—such as textbooks and visual aids—that will be used within classrooms. Decisions on resources as well as teaching strategies employed remain at the discretion of the state, local school board, school, or classroom teacher. *Therefore it is inaccurate for anyone to say that Common Core is usurping local control of the school system.* Individual governors requested this document but their state retains total control of the curriculum and resources used in classrooms.

COMMON CORE IS ALREADY EVIDENT

The current debate concerning Common Core is actually superfluous and likely motivated to achieve political purposes. There is already a de facto common set of standards in place that is used to develop the NAEP assessments in twelve subject areas. States utilize their own curricula while sample groups of their students write these national assessments. *Experts had political authority to develop these assessments,* which receive general endorsement across the nation. Accomplishing their task required that outcomes be articulated within each subject for the grades involved.

The significant issue emerging with Common Core pertains to the change from a representative sample of students across all states to an assessment program for all students. While some exceptions apply for students with special needs, the expectation is that all students in grades 3–8 and one grade in high school will be assessed relative to the standards identified in Common Core. Specificity in measuring student achievement is greatly enhanced and can be monitored to the level of specific teachers. Accountability for all is magnified! The angst generated is understandable.

This entire situation involving common standards is also comparable to the *international testing programs* operated by OECD through PISA and the TIMSS and PIRLS assessments, which have consulted with the nations of the world regarding student outcomes—or standards—expected by specific ages or grade levels. The United States participates in these international assessments and there is no concern being expressed that control of the curriculum outcomes is lost. Assessment of student achievement is based on the standards identified by the consortium of countries participating in the testing program.

American students are now writing standardized tests developed by a consortium of nations. Information gleaned from these assessments provides the individual states, as well as the country overall, with information on how student learning compares with other states and countries. These test results provide governments with an understanding of whether their education strategies are working, as well as where there may be places in the world from which they can learn. The benefit is only feasible because students from all participating regions write the same test and, as noted in chapter 1, American students are not performing at a high level compared with those in comparator nations.

This example from international assessments exposes another issue that some Americans express as sufficient reason to oppose Common Core. Their claim is that the Common Core implies bringing all states down to the lowest common denominator or, in other words, that already high-performing states are taking a step down by accepting these new standards. In fact, the opposite is true. The governors agreed that no state would lower its standards. In other words, this new set of standards would be modernized to accompany what today's world demands of children preparing to enter adulthood and, specifically, the workplace.

Data is already presented that demonstrates low levels of achievement by American students on international assessments. The new standards are not crafted to maintain the low U.S. ranking, but rather to equip students with necessary skills and abilities commensurate with the Race to the Top initiative. While a few states have performance levels near the highest performing countries in the world, all states can have their students achieving at higher levels.

The purpose of this chapter is to debunk myths that have emerged and confused the public regarding Common Core. It is not a curriculum, and the federal government is not involved in its design. Rather, it is developed by a consortium of states for the purpose of raising levels of student achievement across participating states. What was designed as a concept commensurate with the Constitution is misconstrued to create doubt in the public's mind.

Confusion regarding this issue is an example of how rumor and innuendo can disrupt an important facet in our society such as education. Many political leaders did not do a good job of communicating the facts to their electorate so that it was clear that Common Core was both designed and controlled by the states. It is likely that politicians have ulterior motives around appealing to special-interest groups that prevent them from making an effort to ensure that aspects of Common Core are clearly enunciated. The complexities of issues in education are seldom understood and this book endeavors to clarify many nuances lurking in the background surrounding Common Core.

The key points made in this chapter are as follows:

- The terms *Common Core* and *curriculum* are not synonymous.
- Curriculum is the mandate of the state and local school boards.

- Common Core is developed by a consortium of states and, therefore, some control at the individual state level is lost voluntarily.
- We are in a global village, and it is not surprising that states are banding together to pursue a common set of standards.
- Common Core is already evident in national and international assessments.
- Governors agreed that no state would lower its standards and Common Core would be modernized to accomplish what today's world demands.

FOUR

The Political Game

Let us not seek the Republican answer or the Democratic answer, but the right answer. Let us not seek to fix the blame for the past. Let us accept our own responsibility for the future.

—John F. Kennedy

In politics stupidity is not a handicap.

—Napoleon Bonaparte

The whole aim of practical politics is to keep the populace alarmed (and hence clamorous to be led to safety) by menacing it with an endless series of hobgoblins, all of them imaginary.

—H. L. Mencken

One of the reasons people hate politics is that truth is rarely a politician's objective. Election and power are.

—Cal Thomas

The first resistance to social change is to say it's not necessary.

—Gloria Steinem

George Washington is the only president who didn't blame the previous administration for his troubles.

—Author Unknown

Since the advent of Common Core on the scene of American education, it has become an issue discussed widely in political circles at all levels (local, state, and federal) as well as in homes by families. The pithy political proclamations above partly portrayed the environment surrounding Common Core prior to the 2016 election campaign and when political rhetoric was heating up.

For presidential candidates in the Republican Party, Common Core was an important campaign issue with the media as they endeavored to separate these candidates into various ideological camps. When the veneer is scratched away and truth is unpacked, *the candidates' political rhetoric was more emotion than common sense.*

This book already exposes how two concepts are misrepresented in the Common Core discussion. This is not an example of federal government overreach; rather it is a concept *precipitated by forty-five governors* who wanted to raise standards for all of their states above what already exists in any one state.

Second, standards, a federal role, should not be confused with curriculum, a local responsibility. *States can follow whatever curriculum they choose as well as the resources for use in the classroom.* Republican and Democratic governors agreed that their students would be assessed against world-class standards similar to what already occurs when countries participate in international tests and when states participate in NAEP.

Truth was sacrificed in the political debate as candidates pursued *election and power.* As usual, Republican and Democratic camps blurred the debate as to what might be in the nation's best interests, and some Republicans were particularly focused on *spreading alarm.* They confused the issue by claiming that Common Cure was synonymous with common curriculum: a state mandate.

On the other hand, some Democrats were concerned that accountability through assessment is not necessary, even though Republicans often clamor for it—but not this time. While teachers' unions supported Common Core, linking this accountability initiative with common assessment crossed a line. Incorporating student achievement into teacher evaluations, which then provided a basis for paying teachers, was offensive to teachers.

Teachers comprise one of the largest groups in the nation's workforce, which makes them a powerful political force. Their longstanding support of Democrats kept several key candidates from siding with the Common Core initiative unless it was uncoupled from common assessment.

Napoleon was right when he called it all "stupid," and the debate was overshadowed by people—especially educators—wanting to *lay blame on the previous administration* when President Bush introduced NCLB. They conveniently overlook that this accountability program from the federal government was supported by Democrats and, especially, Senator Ted Kennedy, who coauthored the legislation.

POLITICIZATIONS OF COMMON CORE

Several Republican candidates for president were governors who will have understood the differentiation of powers between the state and federal governments. Three governors (Bush, Christie, and Jindal) actually signed the original documents requesting development of Common Core documents. Of these, Bush remained committed, although he perceived a need to downplay his support because of opposition to Common Core from other candidates. Kasich, while not an original signatory, was a strong proponent who believed that *Common Core was actually common sense.*

A prevalent perception voiced by many candidates was that Common Core was a curriculum even though it was not. Fearmongering that the federal government was attempting to implement a national curriculum was a common theme at a time when Republican candidates were appealing to a sentiment focused on local control rather than "big government." Thomas's point that "truth is rarely a politician's objective" was definitely evident whenever discussion focused on the origin of Common Core.

Some candidates understood how the common standards differed from curriculum but demonstrated their opposition toward commonality by promising to build a document with even higher standards. Their intentions were to continue with the common assessments being developed for Common Core, but separation from any association with another state was deemed necessary for projecting an image that they controlled the state's destiny. Reviews of these independent efforts revealed remarkable similarities with the Common Core documents.

Another creative solution emerged as politicians toyed with notions of introducing flexibility through a variety of opting-out provisions. Permitting these escape mechanisms for schools and districts to opt out of the testing provisions negates the common standards approach because accountability for teaching these is removed. Similarly, when parents have been influenced to withdraw their children from the common assessments, evidence that the common standards are being taught may be compromised to the degree that we are uncertain that Common Core is actually implemented.

In all of the rhetoric surrounding Common Core during the 2016 presidential election, we must acknowledge that the federal government's NCLB played a significant role in American education. Even though states controlled their own standards and assessments, NCLB provided the basis for consequences. Rewards and sanctions based on performance were supported initially by both parties, and this initiative continued for more than a decade. Accountability within education may have had its controversies but efforts to remove this program launched by the federal government remained politically problematic.

The Common Core State Standards are an example of states recognizing a problem, then working together, sharing what works and what does not. This initiative fixes the problem evident in NCLB where states merely reduced their standards to achieve rewards. Governors likely recognized this manipulation when they compared student achievement against other benchmarks such as international and NAEP assessments. In essence, they trumped NCLB by approving common standards for their states.

During the preliminary events leading to the 2016 elections, some politicians changed their position as political intensities increased. Some critics may argue that a change in position shows inconsistent principles or lack of backbone while others see it as pragmatism or willingness to compromise.

Candidates usually agree on 90 percent of the issues and differences usually are the areas candidates attempt to exploit (Brown 2015). Loveless (2015) observed that "[Common Core] will be a major issue because of its symbolic importance. It's red meat for the kinds of conservative activists that a number of the contenders on the Republican side want to appeal to." Indeed, many presidential candidates withdrew or denied support so that their financial aid and voting support from these groups did not migrate away on the basis of Common Core.

At the same time, the business community, including the Chamber of Commerce and the Business Round Table, supported Common Core, and candidates struggled to gain their endorsement while conducting their retreat from Common Core. Further, there were supporters beyond the business community. Petrilli (2015) reported a message from Bill Bennett (secretary of education under former president Ronald Reagan): "But these sound academic standards are worth fighting for. Let's go back to the original, conservative understanding of Common Core."

Other groups also had interest in this issue and a potential to determine its future when they entered the polling booth. Wolfgang (2015) reports that an NBC News "State of Parenting" survey released in April 2015, showed that *73 percent of Hispanic parents and 56 percent of black parents viewed Common Core favorably, compared with 41 percent of white parents.* The poll also found that 61 percent of Democrats and 57 percent of independents back Common Core, compared with 26 percent of Republicans.

Herein was a major dilemma for Republican candidates. According to Grier's (2012) review of the 2012 presidential election exit polls,

> Democratic president Obama won 93 percent of African-Americans, 71 percent of Hispanics, and 73 percent of Asians. Mitt Romney, meanwhile, won about 59 percent of the white vote. That's the best a GOP nominee has done among whites since 1988. . . . It's clear that Hispanics are quickly becoming a political force that national politicians must acknowledge. They increased their share of the electorate by about three percentage points; at that pace, they'll tie or pass African-Americans as the largest minority voting bloc in 2016.

Raising achievement levels of minority students is a key attribute of Common Core. Undoubtedly their parents could consider presidential candidates' perspectives on this issue when entering the polling booth; however, politics can be fickle and voters easily swayed by issues emerging during the final weeks before the election.

Prior to the 2016 election, early comments from the list of presidential candidates demonstrated how ill prepared many were regarding the facts and implications of a significant educational issue. Once out of the starting blocks when articulating beliefs about the initiative, many candidates functioned like a contortionist seeking to reshape their position. Alignment with key constituents is a significant matter in getting elected, and several candidates invented "wiggle room" making it appear that they were no longer fully endorsing Common Core.

At the core of the problem was the poor job that states which participated in Common Core did in preparing their citizens, especially parents. Delinquent in providing leadership for a successful transition toward higher standards forced many politicians into damage control. These adjustments required that words and actions be carefully choreographed to avoid offending both supporters and those who eventually might be. A casual observer could find the political gamesmanship humorous if Winston Churchill had been wrong when he said, "Politics is not a game. It is earnest business."

The key points made in this chapter are as follows:

- Presidential candidates were poorly prepared regarding Common Core.
- Many Republican candidates for president sought right-wing voter support by backtracking from their previous support for Common Core.
- Democrats, with only one significant contender for the office of president in the early stages, were relatively silent about Common Core.
- Key groups such as business and ethnic minorities support Common Core.

FIVE

Trust or Accountability

Our world is vastly different today than it was a few generations ago. Living conditions did not change much from generation to generation and, perhaps, from one millennium to the next. Basically, *people worked more with their hands than with their heads.* The central focus for most was finding their own food and shelter so they might exist for three or four decades. There were few options and opportunities for acquiring material possessions and climbing to a higher rung in society. In simple terms, life was about family and trying to survive.

Schooling existed for only a few and was aimed primarily toward teaching reading so that people could read religious documents. In the United States, government-supported *free* public schools for all did not begin until after the American Revolution. Later, states passed laws making schooling *compulsory,* beginning with Massachusetts in 1852 and culminating with Mississippi in 1917.

Heraclitus, a Greek philosopher of Ephesus who was active around 500 BC, propounded a distinctive theory that "change is the only constant in life." He would likely be in awe at the pace of change evident in the twentieth century, which continues to this day. Communication is instant; travel time is measured in minutes and hours rather than weeks and months; family relationships are much more complex; and so on. Education is now a significant component in our society even to the extent that it is one of the major aspects of political activity. Certainly it is one of the major budget areas in government spending.

CHANGES IN AMERICAN CULTURE

From a social perspective, a significant change in our world is evident in the average life span of citizens. Whereas life expectancy for Americans in 2007 was seventy-eight years of age, in 1900 it was only forty-seven years: an increase of 66 percent in slightly more than a century. In that bygone era, when people lived for a shorter period of time, most voting adults with children had a relatively recent experience with the school system: mainly because they did not live very long.

Involvement and interactions usually breed trust, and parents knew their child's teachers not only within the walls of the school building but also within the borders of their community. Formal surveys were uncommon a few decades ago; however, anecdotal evidence suggests that the close relationships between the community and teachers at the school provided for higher levels of trust between the home and school in particular and between voters and educators in general.

The twentieth century also was a time when the American family was significantly smaller than was the case in the 1800s, when many families were part of an agrarian society. For example, in 1800 there were seven children per family but this ratio was reduced to half—that is 3.5—by 1900. Nowadays, the fertility rate in the United States is between two and three children. The need to have children work declined with the demise of the agrarian society and the emergence of the Industrial Age. *Fewer children in the family also shortens the period of years when parents are involved directly with the school system.*

Larger farms combined with the introduction of machinery to work the farm necessitated fewer farmers. As people flocked to the cities, raising children was more costly when the family lived in an urban setting rather than on a farm. Whereas producing food for a family living on a farm was relatively inexpensive, living in a city on a relatively small plot of land made growing food for the family virtually impossible.

From an educational perspective, *trust in the nation's school system has waned.* Fewer children in the family combined with people living much longer lives means there is a significant decline in the percentage of voters with recent, ongoing interaction with schools. Lack of familiarity is not helpful for developing positive perspectives. Davis and Smith (1994) reported that "increasingly, Americans distrust their educational institutions and the people who work in them. This distrust reflects a belief that schools are inadequately fulfilling their responsibilities to educate the nation's children to be productive citizens."

Gallup, on its website, demonstrates a declining level of confidence in the nation's schools. In 2004, only 41 percent of the population indicated a "great deal" or "quite a lot" of confidence in schools. In 2009, this level of confidence declined to 38 percent but has now plummeted to 26 percent in 2014. This more recent substantial decline in confidence levels is likely related to the public's confusion regarding Common Core, which underscores why this book is so relevant.

Confidence in the education system also declined because of information pertaining to educational outcomes released in the latter part of the twentieth century, resulting in the *Nation at Risk* report. This critical report of the education system solidified an understanding for many Americans that their schools required some check and balance processes. *Trust has to be earned, and reports from international assessments are not encouraging.*

From a political perspective, teachers' unions, which have emerged as powerful forces in educational politics, are exacerbating the situation. People are now more likely to understand that *unions are there to support the best interests of their members.* The controversy surrounding these unions is whether they are a stumbling block to reform or advocates for better schools and better teachers. Public attitudes regarding this differing perspective are shifting. Peterson et al. (2012) asked Americans, "Do you think teachers' unions have a generally positive effect on schools, or do you think they have a generally negative effect?"

While 41 percent of the public selected the neutral position, those with a positive view of unions dropped to 22 percent in 2012 from 29 percent in 2011. The survey question is loaded with conflicting values that likely influence such a high rate of uncertainty with the two out of five Americans who indicated a neutral position. There may also be some ambivalence because many Americans do not have a recent connection with the school system and, in their minds, rephrased the "neutral" option as "I don't know."

The survey's most striking finding was "that 58 percent of teachers took a positive view of unions in 2011, and only 43 percent in 2012. The number of teachers holding negative views of unions nearly doubled to 32 percent from 17 percent." A change of this magnitude in one year must be a substantial concern to union leadership. Initially, unions supported Common Core, but, as the focus shifted from student outcomes to using test results on these outcomes in teacher evaluations, were teachers telling their unions to back away? *Everyone wants a higher level of public sector accountability until it enters their own backyard.*

Skepticism toward teachers' unions is also voiced by high-profile people in government. With concerns regarding failing schools running high, Jerry Adler (2010), a writer for *Newsweek*, coordinated a debate about the role that America's unions play and their image of being intransigent while defending every teacher. Rod Paige, former U.S. education secretary, provided his blunt assessment of teachers' union power:

> Teachers' unions represent the most dominant political force in American education—highly financed, highly organized, mammoth organizations. The National Education Association has 3.2 million members, 14,000 locals, and in 2007 they collected about $400 million from their members. In America about 12 percent of the workforce is unionized, but in education it's 38 percent. Teachers' unions sit on both sides of the negotiating table in many cases. They have representatives on the school boards, so they're negotiating with themselves. You heard a lot about children. Don't be fooled: teachers unions' main interest is the welfare of their members.

Paige not only underscores the perception that unions are there for their members (and not for their clients) but also raises the specter of a conflict of interest where people with direct ties to education sit on school boards. *Governments and their citizens pay dearly for their unwillingness to confront this irregularity.*

The unions are not oblivious to their declining support. Members may feel less enchanted about their union leadership, but those in charge are inclined to trumpet their success in wielding political power. At his retirement speech in 2009, the former general counsel for the National Education Association, Bob Chanin, said,

> I have found it increasingly necessary to spend time defending NEA and its affiliates against attacks from government agencies, conservative and right-wing groups and unfriendly media. Why you may ask is this so? Why are these conservative and right-wing bastards picking on NEA and its affiliates? I will tell you why. It is the price we pay for success. NEA and its affiliates have been singled out because they are the most effective union in the United States. . . . It is not because we care about children. And it is not because we have a vision of a great public school for every child. NEA and its affiliates are effective advo-

cates because we have power. And we have power because there are more than 3.2 million people who are willing to pay us hundreds of millions of dollars in dues each year.

But would teachers pay dues if not required to do so? In Wisconsin, where Governor Scott Walker removed compulsory membership, since June 2011, teacher enrollment in National Education Association dropped nearly one-third from almost 100,000 members, while the membership of the American Federation of Teachers fell by more than one-half.

Black (2013), an example of one of Chanin's "unfriendly media," looks at the other side of this coin and succinctly described how unionization progressed successfully into the public sector.

> For many years, the often explicit understanding was that public employees would be less well-paid than those in the private sector, but would have greater job security and, in general, less challenging employment. The unionization of the public service consigned that rule of thumb to the proverbial dust-bin of history, and public-service unions began leading organized labour in militancy, while feasting on the weakness and cowardice of political employers. . . . It is now a familiar three-hanky tear-jerker to see teachers' union representatives passionately explaining that the last thing they wish to do by striking in the middle of the school year is hold the students hostage or impinge on the money-earning capacity of their parents; but that is, of course, what they are doing and why they are doing it.

The point is that trust in the education system is declining because of a variety of factors, not least of which is low levels of student achievement relative to other countries as well as disparate levels of student learning evident between states within the United States. Also evident is how political forces within education are impacting negatively in an area within our culture that, at one time, enjoyed high levels of trust. The Common Core initiative, and the discussion it generates, is contributing to public awareness that education reform is necessary.

DECLINING PUBLIC TRUST IN GOVERNMENT

While many factors within the United States conspired to diminish trust in the school system, there is also the reality that loss of trust in government services is a global trend. In short, if government is involved, there is likelihood of public mistrust. A presentation from June 3, 2009, by

Globescan to a group of government officials demonstrates how seriously trust in the government has declined. In 1964, Globescan reported that 77 percent of the American public indicated they trusted the government. By 1980 only 26 percent admitted this. While it rose to 43 percent in 1984, it bounced between 20 percent and 30 percent since 1990 and 2006.

At this point, it is worthwhile to provide greater context for this loss of trust. Globescan conducted four surveys between 2001 and 2005 in fourteen countries—Argentina, Canada, France, Germany, Great Britain, India, Indonesia, Italy, Mexico, Nigeria, Russia, Spain, Turkey, and the United States. Globescan obtained a net rating of averages across these countries by subtracting non-trust from trust and comparing the result with other significant groups. The net ratings are as follows:

- nongovernmental organizations (+29)
- United Nations (+13)
- large local companies (+2)
- *national governments (-9)*
- global companies (-15)

By 2006, North American trust levels had a dramatically negative impact on the average for the group of fourteen countries. With only approximately 30 percent of citizens in both Canada and the United States reporting "trust" in the government, the net rating was at approximately a minus forty level. *The North American average for distrust of its government is a serious issue as we watch politicians borrow today so that they have a better chance of being elected tomorrow.* Then, at some future time, they retire, leaving the citizenry (more specifically, the children) to deal with the debts incurred by their reelection efforts. Bluntly stated, *this is failing leadership that is producing an unconscionable situation.*

This study is important because education is big business and one of the major expenses in any state budget. Where a society invests its money is also a sign of what it values. While the public has lost faith in its politicians, there is an even greater risk for greater loss of trust if a continued erosion of public goodwill occurs and turmoil develops in the education system.

A large portion of the adult population relies on its school system to function normally without disruption. When a tumultuous period of labor negotiations with teachers begins, the public generally throws support behind the teachers even though the governance body is supposed to represent the public's best interests. *The general public pays for the level of distrust now directed toward government.*

These are a few examples regarding how social, educational, and political factors contribute to the waning trust in the nation's school system. Other significant examples will emerge during discussion of major issues in subsequent chapters. The point is that many factors are conspiring to reduce public confidence and some transformational change is necessary to reverse this undesirable trend. Change may produce levels of discomfort within education's special interest groups; however, politicians are now motivated to initiate necessary reforms.

EDUCATION AND EMPLOYMENT

When the overwhelming list of state governors made the decision to launch Common Core, they triggered opportunity for rebuilding trust in the school system by providing all American students with a more fair education. *The disparate results in student achievement across America outlined earlier are not defensible.* Students in every region of the country must benefit from high standards so that all states can benefit from high rates of employment and economic well-being.

For example, chapter 2 presented a list of student achievement by state on the 2012 international PISA tests. Of the ten states achieving the highest test scores for mathematics and reading, eight states were in both lists—Massachusetts, Minnesota, Vermont, New Jersey, Montana, New Hampshire, South Dakota, and Pennsylvania. Coincidentally, there were also eight states out of the lowest ten in both lists recording the lowest levels of student achievement—District of Columbia (identified as a state for this analysis), New Mexico, Mississippi, Louisiana, Hawaii, Alabama, Nevada, and West Virginia.

Connecting these two lists of high- and low-achieving students with March 2015 State Unemployment Rates, a definite relationship is evident between student achievement and unemployment. In the eight states with high-achieving students in mathematics and reading, unemployment was 4.45 percent. Conversely, in the eight states with low-achieving students in these two subjects, unemployment was 6.64 percent, or 50 percent higher. *Fortunately, all of these states with high rates of unemployment are participants in the Common Core initiative.*

Comparisons of this nature provide lawmakers with necessary impetus to take additional steps, and there is a logical follow-up initiative occurring with implementation of Common Core. Recall that the governors want to establish a common set of high standards for students in their states. There is no stipulation regarding need for a common curriculum or classroom learning resources; rather, learning outcomes are the focus. This distinction bears repeating because of the many voices in the public arena seeking to discredit Common Core as overreach by the U.S. Department of Education.

REBUILDING TRUST IN EDUCATION

With public trust in the education system waning there is a concomitant thrust for increased accountability. The public wants and deserves to know that their tax dollars are preparing today's students with fair opportunity to be successful in tomorrow's world. We are constantly reminded that education is the key to future well-being, but *our indicators of success are demonstrating that more than trust is necessary.* Our solution to waning trust is to introduce accountability for results.

The advent of common standards is a logical pre-condition for increasing accountability through common assessment. When the 45 states applied for funding to participate in the Race to the Top initiative, the stage was set to close the loophole existing within the NCLB program. Funded by the 2009 American Recovery and Reinvestment Act (ARRA) and commonly referred to as the Stimulus or the Recovery Act, RttT supported the states by establishing two pilot programs for assessing student achievement; however, their selection requires additional understanding regarding their purpose.

As explained earlier in this book, NCLB attempted to motivate improvement in the nation's schools receiving Title 1 grants by rewarding them for meeting Adequate Yearly Progress (AYP) targets. The objectives must be set with the goal of having all students at the proficient level or above within twelve years (i.e., by the end of the 2013–2014 school year). *The act requires states to develop assessments in basic skills.* To receive federal school funding, states must give these assessments to all students at select grade levels. *The act does not assert a national achievement standard, and each individual state develops its own standards.*

Title I, Part A of the Elementary and Secondary Education Act (ESEA), as amended, provides financial assistance to local educational agencies (LEAs) and schools with high numbers of children from low-income families to help ensure that all children meet challenging state academic standards. Federal funds are currently allocated through four statutory formulas that are based primarily on census poverty estimates and the cost of education in each state.

Title I schools with at least 40 percent of students from low-income families may use Title I funds, along with other federal, state, and local funds, to operate a school-wide program to upgrade the instructional program for the whole school. Title I schools with less than the 40 percent school-wide threshold or that choose not to operate a school-wide program offer a "targeted assistance program" in which the school identifies students who are failing, or most at risk of failing, to meet the state's challenging academic achievement standards.

Dillon and Rotherham (2009) explain that NCLB requires all public schools receiving federal funding to administer a *state-wide standardized test annually to all students*. This means that all students take the same test under the same conditions. Schools that receive Title I funding through the Elementary and Secondary Education Act of 1965 must make Adequate Yearly Progress (AYP) in test scores (e.g., each year, fifth graders *must do better* on standardized tests than the previous year's fifth graders). *The key aspect in this approach is that the measure is improvement rather than raw score, which can be influenced by socioeconomic conditions.*

If the school's results are repeatedly poor, then steps are taken to improve the school:

- Schools that miss AYP for a *second consecutive year* are publicly labeled as *in need of improvement* and must develop a two-year improvement plan for the subject that the school is not teaching well. Students have the option to transfer to a better school within the school district, if any exists.
- Missing AYP in the *third year* forces the school to offer free tutoring and other supplemental education services to struggling students.
- If a school misses its AYP target for a *fourth consecutive year*, the school is said to require "corrective action," which might involve wholesale replacement of staff, introduction of a new curriculum, or extending the amount of time students spend in class.

- A *fifth year of failure* results in planning to restructure the entire school; the plan is implemented if the school fails to hit its AYP targets for the *sixth year in a row*. Common options include closing the school, turning the school into a charter school, hiring a private company to run the school, or asking the state office of education to run the school directly.

Linn et al. (2002) summarize how states must create AYP objectives consistent with the following requirements of the law:

1. States must develop AYP state-wide measurable objectives for improved achievement by all students and for specific groups: economically disadvantaged students, students with disabilities, and students with limited English proficiency.
2. The objectives must be set with the goal of having all students at the proficient level or above within twelve years (i.e., by the end of the 2013–2014 school year).
3. AYP must be based primarily on *state assessments*, but must also include one additional academic indicator.
4. The AYP objectives must be assessed at the school level. Schools that failed to meet their AYP objective for two consecutive years are identified for improvement.
5. School AYP results must be reported separately for each group of students identified above so that it can be determined whether each student group met the AYP objective.
6. At least 95 percent of each group must participate in state assessments.
7. States may aggregate up to three years of data in making AYP determinations.

"The devil is in the details" is a well-known saying, and it is certainly applicable to NCLB. Coupled with another frequently used expression—"accountability without consequences is not accountability"—the initiative provides a comprehensive plan for leveraging school improvement. Consequences are evident throughout the private sector but seldom experienced in the public sector, and certainly not in education beyond matters related to financial impropriety or culpable behavior.

NCLB faced strong opposition soon after its implementation. Criticism from within the education system can be readily summarized using a report on the *FairTest Examiner* (April 2007) wherein discussion focused on burgeoning support for a joint statement from stakeholders criticizing NCLB:

> Testifying before the Joint House-Senate Education Committee, AFT [American Federation of Teachers] President Edward J. McElroy stressed one of the Joint Statement's major critiques of NCLB: The system "misidentifies as failing thousands of schools that are making real progress. Students, parents, teachers, and communities know that their schools are making solid academic progress, yet they're told that they're not making the grade. It's devastating and demoralizing.

The union president's comment regarding "students, parents, teachers, and communities know that their schools are making solid academic progress" typifies educator reactions to many criticisms. By 2007, NCLB was definitely demonstrating that student learning across the nation was not increasing commensurate with AYP. Perhaps the difference in perception is rooted in the union president's reference to "making solid academic progress."

NCLB is not satisfied with making the *usual level of progress* to which educators and parents are accustomed. Already many children are falling behind and simply moving forward under the guise of social promotion. This ill-conceived practice will be discussed in more detail later, but suffice it to say here that it is an academic strategy practiced in many schools that avoids accountability.

Instead, NCLB is demanding higher expectations for the education system, and these expectations are incremental. Maintaining a level of progress for too many American students that is already deficient relative to expectations is no longer acceptable. In other words, students must improve in year one and improve more in year two. More students can and must achieve grade-level expectations. The union president merely uses common educator rhetoric without providing evidence to substantiate the claim, and these *empty claims are the reason why NCLB was crafted to include consequences.*

Or, perhaps he was victimized like so many by the gaming strategy employed by many states once they discovered that AYP was not going to be achieved. Figure 2.1 provides the visible evidence of how gains in student achievement were manipulated in many states by merely reducing standards on their state tests. As unconscionable as this approach appears, people will resort to all sorts of strategies to avoid consequences emanating from poor performance. *This fraudulent approach of reducing the*

difficulty of examinations taken by many states is sufficient reason to ensure that
future assessments occur across many states.

In another report a few years later, Guggino and Brint (2010) summarized perceptions from a contingent of teachers in Riverside, California, who were designated "highly accomplished":

> The legislation fundamentally changed teaching and education in U.S. schools by requiring annual testing of school children and "adequate yearly progress" for every subgroup of students. The act also requires schools to provide after-school tutoring and other services for poor-performing students and mandates that schools hire only "highly qualified" teachers.

The researchers conducted an online survey in 2007 of educators who are National Board Certified Teachers, a rigorous certification process that requires candidates to demonstrate high levels of subject matter knowledge, pedagogical knowledge, and classroom effectiveness by means of performance-based assessment. Guggino and Brint asked these teachers to assess the impact of No Child Left Behind in three areas of professionalism—technical areas of practice, the service ethic of teaching, and professional commitment.

Although few teachers surveyed were enthusiastic supporters, large minorities credited the act with increasing focus on core skills, encouraging planning and organization of lessons, and creating higher expectations for student performance. However, 84 percent of these highly accomplished teachers reported overall unfavorable attitudes toward the act, which is consistent with previous studies, the researchers said.

"Their criticisms focused on concerns about individualized student learning, declining creativity in the classroom, weakened relationships between teachers and students, and the lack of understanding and respect for the skills and experience of teachers," Guggino and Brint said in the report titled "Does the No Child Left Behind Act Help or Hinder K–12 Education?" "These highly accomplished teachers were skeptical, and in some cases angry, about the consequences of No Child Left Behind for the nation's school children. This is a problematic outcome of the legislation, if only because these are precisely the teachers the public schools can least afford to lose."

There is no doubt that NCLB changed the culture of education in the United States. After decades of trust followed by a period of dissatisfaction and skepticism, a new era emerged characterized by increasing expectations using measures of outcome rather than input. Many educators believe that the more appropriate method for evaluating the school system is measuring how much money government spends. Incorporating a few outcome measures, such as graduation rates, seemed reasonable, especially since *the performance of individual educators could not be personally tied to such an outcome.*

When an outcome was attached to a school, accountability for performance was only applicable to high schools. All other schools in the system escaped notice because their students were too young to be incorporated into the data on graduation rates. Transitioning to a culture where consequences are applied to schools throughout the education system and with a focus specifically on student achievement determined by standardized testing presented, to many educators, too dramatic a shift in accountability. Anxiety from this shift soon translated into strong opposition, if not hostility.

A WATERSHED MOMENT FOR EDUCATION

NCLB was a watershed initiative in U.S. education and, perhaps, in the world of education. Government's usual role was to identify a need, develop a program to address that need, and then allocate funds to implement the program. Once implemented, few politicians dared remove a program because there were always special interest groups—including those employed within the initiative—ready to defend its continuation. In NCLB, government adopted bizarre behavior. This initiative was not another "cash cow" for schools and school districts. Something is required for money to flow: improvement!

Although NCLB received bipartisan support initially, it did not take long for educators to express their opposition. Instead of receiving money upfront, funds were generated when student achievement, measured by state standardized tests, actually improved. The normal attitude exhibited by educators was "just give us the damn money!" Asking people to improve performance and then rewarding their stewardship so that they could achieve higher performance in the future was too much beyond the norm.

Many politicians, especially Democrats, abandoned ship when the educator complaints gathered momentum. It was overlooked that states fund basic education and NCLB funds were a bonus rewarding effective stewardship. NCLB was aimed at changing a culture in education that was opposed to competition—a concept that reminded educators of a business model and that is antithetical to the way teachers think. Teacher organizations chafe at government support for charter schools or independent schools because they instill a measure of competition *between* schools.

Competition in the NCLB initiative is an entirely different sort. It is not about competing with someone else as normally happens in the world of business. While this type of competition might also be helpful in education, it conflicts with values of cooperation and teamwork espoused by many within the education system. Those educators inclined toward this type of competitive spirit tend to bridle their enthusiasm in front of more reluctant peers.

The type of competition evident in NCLB is personal, and pertains to comparing performance with the past. The central tenant of this initiative is that teachers in classrooms and principals in schools look at previous levels of performance and work to improve. Competition is with one's self. A teacher's mindset might be as follows: "Last year I was able to assist my students by 'X' and this year it will be by 'X+.'" Inherent in this approach is that outcomes can be improved without more money. People have capacity to use creativity and their potential to achieve more.

Notwithstanding the lack of understanding by many in this watershed initiative, grumbling about more funding was a dominant feature during NCLB's early history. Wikipedia provides some of the salient comments depicting the mood of the time:

> Several provisions of NCLB, such as a push for quality teachers and more professional development, place additional demands on local districts and state education agencies. Some critics claim that extra expenses are not fully reimbursed by increased levels of federal NCLB funding. Others note that funding for the law increased massively following passage and that billions in funds previously allocated to particular uses could be reallocated to new uses. Even before the law's passage, Secretary of Education Rod Paige noted ensuring that children are educated remained a state responsibility regardless of federal support:
>
>> Washington is willing to help [with the additional costs of federal requirements], as we've helped before, even before we [proposed NCLB]. But this is a part of the teaching responsibility that each state has. . . . Washington has offered some assistance now. In the

legislation, we have . . . some support to pay for the development of tests. But even if that should be looked at as a gift, it is the state responsibility to do this.

Various early Democratic supporters of NCLB criticize its implementation, claiming it is not adequately funded by either the federal government or the states. Ted Kennedy, the legislation's initial sponsor, once stated, "The tragedy is that these long overdue reforms are finally in place, but the funds are not." Susan B. Neuman, the U.S. Department of Education's former assistant secretary for elementary and secondary education, commented about her worries of NCLB in a meeting of the International Reading Association:

> In [the most disadvantaged schools] in America, even the most earnest teacher has often given up because they lack every available resource that could possibly make a difference. . . . When we say all children can achieve and then not give them the additional resources . . . we are creating a fantasy.

Organizations have particularly criticized the unwillingness of the federal government to "fully fund" the act. Noting that appropriations bills always originate in the House of Representatives, it is true that during the Bush Administration, neither the Senate nor the White House has even requested federal funding up to the authorized levels for several of the act's main provisions. For example, President Bush requested only $13.3 billion of a possible $22.75 billion in 2006.

From a summative perspective, Grissom et al. (2014) report their findings in the following abstract:

> Several recent studies have examined the impacts of No Child Left Behind (NCLB) on school operations and student achievement. We complement that work by investigating the law's impacts on teachers' perceptions of their work environments and related job attitudes, including satisfaction and commitment to remain in teaching. Using four waves of the nationally representative Schools and Staffing Survey, which cover the period from 1994 to 2008, we document overall trends in teacher attitudes across this time period and take advantage of differences in the presence and strength of prior state accountability systems and differences in likely impacts on high- and low-poverty schools to isolate NCLB effects. Perhaps surprisingly, we show positive trends in many work environment measures, job satisfaction, and commitment across the time period coinciding with the implementation of NCLB. We find, however, relatively modest evidence of an impact of NCLB accountability itself. There is some evidence that the law has

negatively affected perceptions of teacher cooperation but positively affected feelings of classroom control and administrator support. We find little evidence that teacher job satisfaction or commitment has changed in response to NCLB.

A key statement in this study is "We find, however, relatively modest evidence of an impact of NCLB accountability itself." The gaming that states did in reducing the standards of their tests *neutralized the watershed perspective of applying consequences for performance.* Allowing states to control the testing program was the initiative's Achilles' heel. Without uniform standards and measurements in place, too much of the initiative's purpose is compromised. Accountability cannot tolerate fudging, and *requiring consistent measurement* is an effective prevention strategy to overcome such fraudulent activity.

Therefore, not only is Common Core necessary for increasing accountability of an education system that is experiencing declining trust, but common assessment is the logical next step. When almost all governors supported initiating high standards in student learning for their states, they also understood the need to measure student achievement consistently. The loophole in NCLB could be closed if the states valued higher levels of accountability. *Shirking common assessment is a sign demonstrating disingenuous commitment to accountability.*

The Race to the Top initiative, funded by the American Recovery and Reinvestment Act of 2009, identified two pilot assessment initiatives. Each of the forty-five governors, their respective education secretaries, and each university president in their state co-signed an application to participate in RttT, which included schedules for an assessment component. Common assessment would begin in grade 3 and progress to examinations in high school, to be launched in 2015.

One of the two consortia of Common Core states use assessments best described as computer-based assessment (CBA). The PARCC—Partnership for Assessment of Readiness for College and Careers—Assessment Consortium comprised the states of Arizona, Arkansas, Colorado, District of Columbia, Florida, Illinois, Indiana, Kentucky, Louisiana, Maryland, Massachusetts, Mississippi, New Jersey, New Mexico, New York, Ohio, Pennsylvania, Rhode Island, and Tennessee. Their approach focuses on computer-based assessments through the year in each grade together with streamlined end-of-year tests.

This approach is similar to a standardized test but, rather than being administered as a paper and pencil test, it is taken on a computer. The central feature of this model is that it is a standardized test given to all students identified in the cohort. The CBA format is used repeatedly in its exact form from one test administration to the next. Precise questions may be altered to mitigate cheating by using equating procedures, which is a well-documented aspect of test construction.

For the purposes of this book, additional details of test construction are not necessary. Suffice it to say that test developers use many strategies to ensure that standardized tests are reliable and valid. Many countries, including the United States, have test developers well versed in developing excellent, large-scale standardized tests.

The second consortium, called the Smarter Balanced Assessment Consortium, comprised thirty-one states focusing on creating "adaptive online exams." Member states included Alaska, California, Connecticut, Delaware, Hawaii, Idaho, Iowa, Maine, Michigan, Missouri, Montana, Nevada, New Hampshire, North Carolina, North Dakota, Oregon, Pennsylvania, South Carolina, South Dakota, U.S. Virgin Islands, Vermont, Washington, West Virginia, Wisconsin, and Wyoming.

This second consortium of states is using a Computer Adaptive Test (CAT) that features standardized test questions but has the capacity to individualize the test. Students respond to a question, and the "engine" adjusts the level of difficulty for subsequent questions based on whether it was answered correctly.

If correct, the next question is more difficult, but it is less difficult if incorrect. By adjusting every question on the basis of the response to the previous question, *CAT becomes an individualized test.* The test's final score is not recorded as the percent correct; rather, the student is scored on a calibrated scale that is used to chart progress. An added feature of the CAT concept is that less time for testing is required because the individualized component zeroes in more quickly on the student's level of learning.

Regardless of the approach taken, large-scale testing across many states is a significant increase in accountability for the American school system. The NCLB initiative is somewhat ironic because groups within the Republican Party are concerned that Common Core is federal government overreach. In reality, based on the fact that the governors requested Common Core, NCLB—introduced by a Republican president—is an example of greater expansion of the federal role in public education through annual testing, annual academic progress, report cards, teacher qualifications, and funding changes.

The central point in this chapter is that American education is shifting a key value since the turn of this century. A public attitude of trust dominated for centuries; however, lower than expected levels of student success required a more demanding approach. Therefore, commensurate with a reduced level of public trust in their education system is a corresponding increase in accountability required of educators. Naturally, many will claim that this transition is going too far and, hence, the change in culture is creating considerable conflict.

There is value in conflict, however. Student learning is mostly the result of efforts undertaken by the school system and support received from the home environment. When achievement levels are not meeting expectations, these two pillars must be assessed. This book is primarily focused on ensuring the attainment of high standards for the school system by adopting Common Core, common assessments, and consequences.

The key points made in this chapter are as follows:

- Education is now a significant component in our society even to the extent that it is one of the major aspects of political activity.
- Trust in the school system is waning in recent decades.
- Fewer children in families shorten the time when parents are involved with their schools.
- People living much longer reduce the number of voters having children in the school system.
- Confidence in the education system also declined because of information pertaining to poor levels of educational outcomes.
- Teachers' unions have negatively impacted the public's trust in education.
- Mistrust in government in general is a rising concern.
- States' levels of student achievement are related to rates of employment.
- Introducing accountability for results is a solution to waning trust.
- NCLB introduced higher levels of accountability including appropriately identified consequences.

- Bipartisan support for NCLB soon was lost when Democrats abandoned the initiative because of teachers' opposition to increased accountability.
- Competition in the NCLB initiative is an entirely different sort because it is with self rather than with others.
- Race to the Top features two types of assessments: computer based (which are standardized) and computer adaptive (which are individualized).

SIX

Fairness? Finally!

The previous chapter outlined how America's education system is progressing into an era of greater accountability. Discomfort accompanies this progression because the transition incorporates a focus on individual teachers and on specific schools. Tightening accountability is too stressful for many within the system and educator backlash is inevitable. Whereas Common Core is reasonably supported within the education system, incorporating a measurement process based on common assessment brings anxiety to all levels within the education system. *At the heart of this reform is ensuring that fairness to students is paramount.*

Some people believe that life is not fair, so leave it be. We see unfairness all around us, which is unavoidable in some instances. The cause may be due to one's birth condition or an accident, or financial downturn, or criminal intent, all of which are beyond our control. We can fret and even begrudge these unfortunate circumstances, but eventually we can choose to move on because life does. Self-pity regarding misfortune only increases despondency and diminishes our ability to achieve.

Some unfairness can be avoided. Educators believe that students with learning disabilities or disadvantages, because of their home environment, can overcome circumstances with appropriate compensatory assistance. In other words, fairness can be achieved by inequitable spending. The altruistic tendency of most educators is to ensure that children leaving the system have all that is necessary to be successful.

Advances in technology can increase fairness. In sports, for example, global positioning systems and "slo-mo" video replay is widely used.

Players and fans are frustrated with a history of officiating mistakes leading to an unfair outcome in games. In baseball, fans can judge the umpire's decision with every pitch by watching the strike zone on the television screen. The pursuit of fairness in sports activities in what is already happening motivates us to do even more. In school, technology provides more opportunity to personalize education so that students are more engaged in their learning.

FAIRNESS TO ALL STUDENTS IS THE GOAL

American education is on the verge of taking a huge stride toward reducing unfairness to its students. It is unfair to have a variable set of standards in same-grade classrooms within the same school. Students will be advantaged or disadvantaged merely in turning right or left into a classroom to a different teacher. Similarly, students within the same school district deserve to have their teachers preparing them for the same high standards. Communities within a city will not tolerate having their school lower its standards relative to expectations of their neighboring classrooms or schools.

Common Core ensures that all students in participating states benefit from having to achieve high standards in learning. The goal is to ameliorate large disparities in standards between states. Implications stemming from this reform are likely as transformative as any since school attendance became mandatory. At last there is recognition that a second-class education is not helpful to the nation.

As meaningful as this possibility may be, all can be lost in the next step. Common Core is only the first step *and must be accompanied by common assessments*. Like hand and glove, these two concepts are inextricably linked. However, the second step is the litmus test that indicates whether the school system is committed to fairness for students across the nation. Already opposition from within the school system regarding common measurement is fierce. A quotation from a letter to the editor, found in a newspaper regarding standardized testing, articulates an attitudinal shift that demonstrates the controversy.

> We need to increase these services [funding for class size and meals for kids] while continuing to strive for more equity in all schools across the state. I urge [the state] to persevere on our progressive path by increasing investment in schools and teachers, removing the competitive

blockades of increased instruction time and standardized tests, and trusting that teachers and the union, backed by academic research, know what is best for our students.

Many educators challenge large-scale testing because they believe it demonstrates government's *lack of trust in their ability to assess students' academic achievement.* They simply want everyone to trust that they got it right. Any suggestion that the teacher's evaluation of students' work is incorrect, in their view, is offensive, demeaning, and tantamount to heresy. Their defensive response to any doubt expressed about their capacity to render accurate assessments is immediate and aggressive.

Politicians, while playing their political game, have their issues with Common Core. Their focus is on capturing votes today rather than undertaking a complex program focusing on ensuring fairness to students in the future. On the other hand, educators want governments to allocate more on education because spending is seen as a better measure than performance on student outcomes. Inevitably, spending more also helps those working in the school system to achieve their more selfish goal: work less and make more.

Many educators feel nervous when faced with proposals to measure their performance. This emphasis on increased accountability represents a challenge to the complete trust that is desired. *Pursuing a strategy of common assessment is a tipping point in the matter of blind trust in educators versus fairness to students.* The reason why this shift is too complex for politicians stems from their fear of alienating a significant percentage of voters when revealing how weak and inconsistent teachers are when assessing student achievement.

Therefore, ensuring that Common Core is linked with common assessment holds politicians' feet to the fire. The outcomes of their decisions can be compared to those of other regions of the country. Similarly, this linkage increases the accountability of educators regarding their work in terms of performance and consistency. Students are the winners and the nation's future well-being is enhanced—a potential that is easily undone if common assessment is not linked with Common Core.

TEACHERS ARE INCONSISTENT IN EVALUATING
STUDENT ACHIEVEMENT

Evaluating student work is a major aspect of being an effective teacher. While it is a legislated requirement, teachers naturally understand the value in constantly assessing student learning so that they can give feedback to the student, report to parents on their child's learning, report to the public on the extent of learning generally, and use the assessment to modify their future instruction. Assessment is so critical that the teacher's skill in evaluating student achievement requires constant verification and ongoing honing. This verification is even more important now that research is demonstrating how poorly prepared teachers are, and how inaccurate are their assessments of student learning.

Teachers and their unions' orchestrated efforts to discredit large-scale testing make it necessary to openly discuss this issue. The proverbial elephant must be brought into the room. Persistent insistence that teacher's marks on student learning are accurate must be verified so that trust is deserved. If the evidence refutes such accuracy, then absolute trust must be replaced with various forms of accountability. *This chapter challenges teachers' capacity to perform consistently accurate assessments of student achievement.*

Richard Phelps, in 2008, addressed a world congress on student evaluation and clearly expressed his findings with these words:

> There is abundant evidence that teachers' marks are a very unreliable means of measurement. A teacher's grades and test scores are far less likely to be generalizable than any standardized tests. If any assessment system uses tests that are not standardized, the system is likely to be unfair to many candidates. We [educators] need standardized tests because each of us is a prisoner of our own limited experiences and observations.

Phelps thus opened a "Pandora's box" by referencing the likelihood for *unfairness*. Using this term to describe inconsistencies in marking provokes a significant backlash from educators. Criticism is one thing, but suggesting that it results in *unfairness toward students* is something they want kept under wraps. During discussions with teachers on this subject, they make it clear that the public's trust should not be jeopardized by demonstrating problems associated with student assessment. The stakes for the teaching profession are too high. Politicians, too, avoid disclosure because there are expectations for them to ensure that all students are treated fairly.

Inconsistent evaluations of student achievement recently surfaced as a major concern in the United Kingdom. Teachers' unions were pressuring their UK government to abandon large-scale testing in favor of trusting teachers' capacity in accurately assessing student achievement. The government established an expert panel to review the issue, and Bevan et al. (2009) recorded the panel's response to the request with the following statement:

> A high level of accountability for each school is beneficial for everyone who has a stake in the education system: pupils, parents, schools and the taxpayer. The fact that we have strong accountability in the education system means that we can confidently devolve a lot of autonomy to schools and invest high levels of trust in teachers and school leaders. It would therefore be misguided to weaken accountability.
>
> The accuracy and consistency of teacher assessment is improving; and whilst there are issues around variability of marking in tests, independently measuring pupils against national standards remains, in our view, the best way of providing objective information on the performance of each pupil and each school.

The implication in this report is that *trust, manifested through increased autonomy, follows accountability*. Blind trust is not useful to anyone. Autonomy needs to be earned.

In the United States, consistency in evaluating student work is a long-standing concern. *The Gale Encyclopedia of Education: School Grading Systems* traced the root of concern regarding marking inconsistencies back to the beginning of the twentieth century. As more children remained in school beyond grade 5, a shift to percentage grading seemed a natural by-product for higher numbers of students. Inconsistent marks on assessments quickly became a concern.

This encyclopedia references a study in 1912 by Starch and Elliott, wherein teachers marked identical English papers. On the first paper, the range of marks was from 64 percent to 98 percent, with a second paper ranging from 50 percent to 97 percent. This finding precipitated a similar study for mathematics, which demonstrated an even greater discrepancy, with marks ranging from 28 percent to 95 percent. It was evident from these early studies that teachers were applying a variety of *personal biases* while marking these papers.

These discrepancies evident when assigning marks to the same answer lead to another methodology for reporting, which made use of scales with larger ranges such as excellent, average, poor, and failing. This shift to ranges in marks was also the genesis for using letter grades A, B, C, D, and F. While these methods reduced variation in grades from the earlier practice of percentages, they did not resolve the problem of teacher subjectivity. These ranges merely masked discrepant marks that were less than twenty to twenty-five percentage points.

ASSESSMENT INCONSISTENCIES AND THE BELL CURVE

Combating these problems led to the introduction of the Bell Curve with its prescribed distribution of scores for each of the letter grades. This *quota system* for each letter grade, also known as "grading on the curve," relieved teachers of the difficult task of having to identify specific learning criteria for each mark range. The focus was on *ranking* students rather than on *rating* their students' learning relative to standards. *In other words, teachers found it relatively easy to place students' papers in a rank order from best to poorest.*

Teachers could readily discern differences in quality of assignments from students *within their class* and, *not* having to apply standards, could assess each student's response relative to others. The difficulty teachers experienced was in assigning a value to the work that was applied consistently by all teachers across the state, through the school district, or even within their own school. Over time, teachers might eventually develop an understanding of expectations for a specific grade and stray from using the quota approach. When this occurred, inconsistencies were magnified because some teachers applied the quota while others focused on the standards.

Unfortunately, subjectivity always remained an issue. The *Gale Encyclopedia* states,

> Negative consequences result when subjectivity translates to bias. This occurs when factors apart from students' actual achievement or performance affect their grades. Studies have shown, for example, *that cultural differences among students, as well as their appearance, family backgrounds, and lifestyles, can sometimes result in biased evaluations of their academic performance. Teachers' perceptions of students' behavior can also significantly influence their judgments of academic performance.* Students

with behavior problems often have no chance to receive a high grade because their infractions over-shadow their performance. These effects are especially pronounced in judgments of boys. Even the neatness of students' handwriting can significantly affect teachers' judgments.

This tendency toward bias and its negative result on fairness to students is the purpose for this chapter and the reason why large-scale testing and anonymous marking are necessary for a fair approach in assessing student achievement. When unfairness is detected, actions designed to ensure fairness must follow.

ASSESSMENT INCONSISTENCIES TODAY

After a century of dealing with this problem of subjectivity in assessment, it remains a dominant issue in education. Webber et al. (2009) summarize their findings as follows:

> Student assessment is a contested educational issue in most of the Western world. . . . Teachers' weak understanding of fair assessment practices appears to be a barrier to student assessment being perceived as a positive educational endeavor. . . . Reporting to stakeholders clearly, accurately, and sensitively is among the most difficult and uncomfortable parts of student evaluation for teachers and, therefore, may result in student achievement not being reliably conducted, interpreted or reported. . . . *Much research suggests that teachers in general are not proficient in student assessment practices in the western world.* . . . Further, principals are not strong in leading assessment and assessment historically has been missing from principal preparation programs.

Assessment is critical in education, and yet it remains so poorly done that professional development conferences for the purpose of upgrading skills flourish. Bob Marzano, an assessment guru, demonstrated the extent of this issue at a conference involving approximately two thousand educators in Atlanta on October 19, 2007. After posting on the screen a student's marks for ten assignments, he requested a final letter grade from conference participants. Amazingly, the range was from 30 percent to 90 percent and provided a clear indication that inconsistency remains a significant barrier for fairness to students.

Harlen (2005) also undertook a systematic review of research on the reliability of teachers' assessment used for summative purposes. He concluded that "the findings of the review by no means constitute a ringing endorsement of teachers' assessment; there was evidence of *low reliability and bias in teachers' judgements."* These biases lead to unfair treatment of students because marks are their currency for obtaining scholarships and entry into universities. *Ultimately, students are winners or losers because of their teachers' specific biases.*

Uniformity, or consistency, when teachers mark student work remains a significant concern *because absolute objectivity is not possible when humans are involved.* In my regional study, consistency between teachers' assessments of student responses while marking system examinations was always monitored. Controls in place for these marking sessions ensure student anonymity and each question is marked by two teachers. When their marks vary by more than one point on a five-point scale, or 20 percent, a third marker is involved.

Extensive training takes place prior to the marking process and markers break from their task twice daily to review their standards by scoring a "reliability review" paper. The group compares individual assessments and discusses reasons for mark variances. *The commitment for achieving consistency is well beyond what occurs within any school because scholarships and placement into prestigious university programs are at stake.*

Even when there is so much effort toward achieving consistency in assessing students' written responses, approximately 25 percent of upper-stream English; 12 percent of upper-stream social studies; and 10 percent of chemistry questions have marks that require a third read. While third reader rates are less for lower-stream courses where stakes for students are somewhat lower, these studies, replicated with similar results during every examination period over many years, reveal how difficult it is to achieve consistency. Simply, *humans experience factors that expose their fallibilities.* Their ability to concentrate is disrupted by fatigue, hunger, noise, and emotional distractions in their lives.

Conspicuous by its absence in educational research is evidence that there is consistency in assessment. Educators and their unions are unable to counter concerns regarding assessment inconsistencies. Until there is evidence that students' work is measured accurately and consistently across the educational system, trust requires a check-and-balance approach such as is provided through *large-scale standardized assessment accompanied by anonymous marking.* Educators need to abandon their self-serving agenda in favor of fairness to students. Politicians need to support students rather than pander to special interests.

Teacher preparation programs are not ameliorating the problem. In my regional studies, new teachers indicate *preparedness for assessing student work as their greatest concern.* Once these teachers enter the school system they are confronted with their weakness. In regions not using standardized testing, there is less likelihood that teacher marks face a sustained challenge from parents. The advent of standardized testing has altered the landscape, and now significant sums of taxpayer funding to school districts are designated for teacher in-service on assessment. The problem is complex, however, and inconsistency remains.

ASSESSMENT INCONSISTENCY AND GRADE INFLATION

As already stated, teachers bring their biases to the assessment process. Inconsistency in assessment is the central issue, but it is *exacerbated by a tendency toward grade inflation.* We can identify it as *inflation* because classroom marks assigned by teachers are *skewed upward rather than in both directions.* Teacher bias toward inflation likely stems from their belief that content was taught; the teacher then assumes more from the student's answer than what should actually be credited. In other words, the *teacher believes what is taught is caught.* So pervasive is this assumption that one superintendent opined that grade inflation in his district is not endemic, but rather pandemic.

The OECD, which administers the tri-annual PISA tests, published a report in 2012 that discussed grade inflation in the United States. Its conclusion was as follows: "While anecdotal evidence on grade inflation abounds, studies on grade inflation in secondary schools are scarce. The existing evidence signals that grade inflation is common and that, at least in the United States, it has been increasing since the 1990s." *This damning summary should send shockwaves to politicians that common assessment with anonymous marking is an urgent requirement that can only be achieved through a Common Core approach.*

This OECD report is also pointing out another significant issue: "studies on grade inflation in secondary schools are scarce." The real message in this statement is that too many school systems do not utilize common exit examinations so that degrees of grade inflation can be uncovered. My regional studies employ exit examinations and demonstrate how highly inflated are marks many students receive from teachers.

An ongoing absence of this data provides fodder to movements wanting to avoid the accountability that accompanies standardized testing. For example, an interview with Sir Ken Robinson—famous for his TED talks—recorded in *Education Week* (May 19, 2015) featured a response to the question, "Your latest book spans case studies of schools across the country. Many schools have instituted innovative new programs to encourage their students' interests. What kind of school climate makes this kind of innovation possible?" Sir Ken replied,

> I think the key to this is that education has to be recognized as a human business. It's a personal process. We're dealing with living human beings in the middle of all of this. They're not statistics or data points. They're not data sets from a test schedule. These are living people with feelings and aspirations and hopes and ambitions and fears and talents, like you and me and everybody else. As soon as you recognize that education is not a processing plant, it's about people, then the whole equation starts to shift around. My argument, really, is that we should be personalizing education, not standardizing it.

Of course learning should be personalized. That is, the pace of learning should be personalized, and students should have a choice of pathways available as they progress toward graduation. A math teacher with forty-five students in his class told how he never taught a lesson to the whole class at the same time. Rather, he taught many lessons every day to individual students at the precise moment when they required instruction. Sometimes he would have another student, who had just learned the concept a few days earlier, teach it to the needy student. The "teaching student" reinforced their learning while the needy student received help from someone who had just successfully encountered a similar need.

Throughout this personalized process, all students still received the same standardized mathematics tests to ensure that they were learning necessary life skills. They just encountered their instructional needs at different times of the class period, month, or school year. Teachers required feedback to ascertain whether the student was learning even when other students were progressing through their completely personalized learning plan.

What Sir Ken and most other people do not understand is that *any test given to one or more students is standardized*. Teachers are constantly giving standardized tests to their students. The question is whether teachers with little familiarity with test design have constructed their classroom tests to high levels of validity and reliability. Are there subjective aspects in the tests that allow results to be influenced by marker bias? This is the "hand and glove" aspect of assessment. *Common Core, supported by professionally constructed common assessments, will strengthen the American education system.*

To what extent is Sir Ken aware of the data story that already exists regarding how poorly some concepts are being taught in our schools, and how much teacher bias can discredit assessments of student achievement? This chapter is dealing with the second part of this question. Educators and politicians responsible for the education system are reluctant to let this information become part of the public record. Complacency is the endgame; therefore, transparency is substantially omitted. Fairness to students is compromised.

Problems emanating from inconsistent marking can also be somewhat muted when marks are inflated and parents receive an unwarranted rosy picture of their child's academic progress. When messages sent home reflect high standing, everyone is happy. More important, there are no complaints, whether these be focused on the quality of teaching or on the effort at learning. The result is that standards decline until something, such as results from standardized tests, happens to challenge the marking system. Politicians, accountable for their education system, want high marks generated during their time in office. One way to achieve high results is to lower standards.

In the United Kingdom, a Durham University study concluded that an "A" grade in 2009 was the equivalent to a "C" grade in the 1980s. The slippery slope has endured for three decades, and people wonder why students appear less prepared for their world of work. According to the *Daily Telegraph*, this trend goes hand in hand with the "all must have prizes" ethos that has dominated education for decades, to the detriment of academic excellence. The newspaper's summative statement was that "these are the effects of grade inflation that has become endemic in public examinations."

Whether it is endemic as suggested by the newspaper or pandemic as suggested by the superintendent, *grade inflation is a serious problem because it is fraudulent.* Thomas and Bainbridge (1997) examined many American school districts and demonstrated how an inconsistent application in standards produces unfairness. In figure 6.1, school "A" students had the

lowest marks of the five schools on the SAT as well as on norm referenced tests in reading and math. Nevertheless, students received high
marks from their teachers and received a collective grade point average
of 3.6.

In school "E," students scored the highest of the five schools on the
external tests but had the lowest grade point average. These authors summarized their overall findings with the following statement:

> It is extremely difficult to explain how the lowest achieving school can
> have a higher grade point average than the higher achieving schools.
> Yet, this same pattern is found in most of the school districts in which
> the authors have conducted School Effectiveness Audits. . . . The con-
> clusion can be drawn that in low achieving schools with high grade
> point averages, expectations are extremely low—just the opposite of
> what research indicates should be done. Having low expectations be-
> gets low achievement. The fraud is that the high grade point average
> gives a false message to the students. Schools which expect little and
> provide high grades, regardless of the level of academic achievement,
> are fraudulent educational systems and should be corrected.

Educational Fraud

SCHOOL	SAT	Norm Referenced Test (%ile)	Norm Referenced Test (%ile)	GRADE POINT
		Reading	Math	
A	750	35	26	3.6
B	900	40	42	3.2
C	990	48	48	2.8
D	1050	58	55	2.6
E	1125	67	74	2.5

Figure 6.1.

In 2009, the *Queen's Journal* at Queens University in Ontario, Canada, demonstrated the extent of grade inflation throughout an entire province. Canada's *National Post* carried a story stating that the prestigious McGill University "has become the first in Canada to insist applicants from Ontario have higher marks than their peers from other provinces to earn admission." Faced with increasing numbers of students seeking entry to a limited number of post-secondary placements, teachers endeavored to give their students an advantage in qualifying for entry by lowering their standards.

McGill University acknowledged that students from Ontario were going to have their grades deflated by 7 percent *to achieve greater fairness for students applying from other provinces*. Ontario's abolition of province-wide exams decades earlier meant that the teacher's mark was the final mark; students registering with an "A" had increased from 18 percent in 1992 to 40 percent in 2007. The *Queen's Journal* editorial concluded that "the number of 'A' students isn't growing because people are getting smarter. Rather, academic standards have declined so it is easier to get an 'A' than ever before—a phenomenon known as grade inflation."

In this report, James Côté, a sociology professor at the University of Western Ontario, wrote:

> Grade inflation creates an education system that hurts students. It differentiates among students less and gives them less feedback on the quality of work. It's generally a dis-incentive for working harder because it really means it's easier to get a higher grade. For the students who deserve the higher grade in the first place it can be demoralizing. . . . It also gives people false feedback that they themselves are above average. They get an inflated view of themselves in terms of who they are and what they can do academically.

He went on to say, "Standardized testing would help curb the problem. . . . We're hesitant to [use standardized tests] in Canada, but it would help."

Of course standardized tests would help! Wikipedia researchers summarized their assessment of this issue as follows:

> In 2007, 40 percent of Ontario high school graduates leave with "A" averages—8 times as many as would be awarded in the traditional British system. In Alberta, as of 2007, just over 20 percent of high school graduates leave with an "A" average. This discrepancy may be explained by the fact that all Alberta high school students must write

province-wide standardized exams, Diploma exams, in core subjects, in
order to graduate.

Canada's University of Saskatchewan conducted a follow-up study in
2011. They found that high school students from Alberta did better academically in their first year at that university than their peers from British
Columbia, Manitoba, Ontario, and Saskatchewan. The study followed
12,000 incoming students over three years and found that Alberta students' grades dropped 6.4 percentage points in their first year at the
university, while students from the four other provinces saw a decrease
of 19.6 percentage points, *three times greater than the province using exit
examinations.*

Alberta is the only one of these five provinces that mandates diploma
examinations. *Through the use of provincial examinations, Alberta's educational system is able to limit the amount of grade inflation in its schools.* There
still is evidence that grade inflation occurs and that it is significant, but
diploma examinations provide a check and balance for greater accuracy
and consistency in assessing student work.

The *University of Saskatchewan* report concluded that the "study also
confirms what many of us in admissions suspected or knew anecdotal-
ly—grade inflation is common and the best students come from Alberta
high schools." A reporter from the *Calgary Herald* (November 28, 2011)
reported on this study, quoting Dr. McQuillan, the University of Calgary's dean of arts, who said, "As admissions become more difficult and
competitive, each school in Ontario tends to say let's give our students a
leg up by giving them higher grades. . . . There's an arms race of A's going on."
Fraud can be so easy to explain away.

While Ontario universities were loath to admit it publicly for fear of
creating controversy, registrars told McQuillan that they were *quietly adjusting the marks for Alberta students to compensate.* This story was followed
up in the *Vancouver Sun* (March 22, 2012), acknowledging that the University of British Columbia "adds two percentage points to the averages
of students applying from Alberta because the grading system is tougher
in that province." Michael Bluhm, UBC's associate director of undergrad-
uate admissions, was quoted as saying:

> We recognize this difference when evaluating Alberta students for ad-
> mission. I'll be clear to state that this is not a boost or benefit, per se, to
> Alberta students over BC students; rather an acknowledgment that the
> two grading systems are different. Alberta is the only province where

we currently see valid and quantifiable data to warrant consideration in our admission decisions.

While Alberta's students experienced less grade inflation than students from other provinces, grade inflation still is evident in their high schools. Figure 6.2 demonstrates an interesting phenomenon: First, the general portrayal in this chart *is replicated annually and in all subjects* where there are two course streams. In this case, Social Studies 30 is the upper-stream course leading to a university program and demonstrates consistently that the school marks from teachers are higher than the Diploma Examination marks for both the Acceptable Standard (passing) and the Standard of Excellence ("A").

For example, in the first year at the chart's left edge, 14 percent more students achieved the Acceptable Standard and 40 percent more achieved the Standard of Excellence from their school than was earned on the Diploma Examination. This pattern of high discrepancies at the Standard of Excellence is a second key aspect, and is important because it is at this standard that scholarships are won and placements in prestigious universities are achieved. Stakes are highest at the Standard of Excellence. The consistency across the years is amazing.

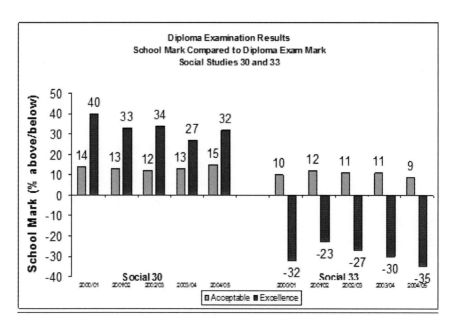

Figure 6.2.

Equally noteworthy is the pattern on the right-hand side of the chart for the lower-stream Social Studies 33. Again, the variances between school generated marks and Diploma Examination scores are consistent from year to year. There is, however, a strange pattern for the Standard of Excellence because Diploma Examination marks are substantially below school generated marks. The explanation comes from interactions with many teachers of the lower-stream courses indicating that they do *not give out "A" marks in lower-stream courses because the student chose the easier stream.*

Teachers believe that students avoided the challenge of taking the more difficult stream. Therefore, teachers exercised their own *bias* in assessing student achievement by *penalizing* them for taking the easier course. In effect, teachers disregarded course standards and applied their own. Not only were these trends evident in social studies, but they were also replicated in mathematics, English, and science. Inaccurate student assessments in classrooms are biased toward inflation except when there is a perceived need to penalize students for not taking on course work that the teachers believe to be more challenging.

In a provincial meeting of school board trustees, an ex-teacher of Social Studies 33 took the podium and reiterated this *penalty* aspect to her colleagues. She openly acknowledged never giving an "A" to students in her course because she felt that students should have registered for the more challenging Social Studies 30 course. Even though students were demonstrating responses to examination questions at the "A" level, *she imposed her biases on students by penalizing their choice in subjects.*

A final aspect of this Alberta study focused on what took place in each school district across the province. Again the pattern was consistent from year to year, with only minor exceptions. Basically, in all school districts, *school generated marks in upper-stream courses were higher than Diploma Examination marks.* If this trend was not indicative of grade inflation, there would be a relatively equal number of districts above and below. Diploma Examinations may provide a check and balance for grade inflation but elimination is not guaranteed; rather, it reduces the potential.

One parent, upon reviewing these disturbing studies, commented on how important it is to ensure consistent standards not only across the country *but also around the world.* She understood that registrars across Canada were adjusting student applicants according to province, but what about students applying for placements in other countries? Her child had applied to Harvard but was not accepted.

Alberta's success at maintaining standards resulted in her child receiving a more accurate set of marks, but this otherwise commendable state of affairs may have penalized her child and, presumably many others, who would otherwise have been accepted into a prestigious university in another country unfamiliar with the high standards in one Canadian province.

A study in Ontario further demonstrates how rampant inflation in the other Canadian provinces can confuse selection processes and impact negatively our preferred objective: fairness to students (Van Wijngaarden 2013). This researcher writes:

> The situation is frustrating for all involved in education. Pressure is exerted on high school teachers to water down curriculum and pass students. In Ontario, universities use the highest six Grade 12 subjects to determine admission and award scholarships. This can mean big bucks. A student having an average over 90 percent can receive a total of $10,000 in scholarships over four years if they maintain an A average. Unfortunately, most first-year university students see their grades plummet. At York University, only about one percent of students entering with a high school average between 80 and 85 percent keep their "renewable" scholarships. . . . An obvious answer is a return to mandatory province-wide exams but that is not politically saleable.

These examples demonstrate the prevalence of grade inflation in many parts of the world, including regions within the United States. A comprehensive analysis across the country is provided in a 2005 report by American College Testing (ACT) titled "Issues in College Readiness: Are High School Grades Inflated?" ACT scores and cumulative high school grade point average (GPA) represent quantitative measures that are typically used by colleges to predict a student's first-semester or first-year college GPA. This report explains how it can detect the presence of grade inflation:

> One factor that is commonly believed to influence the reliability of high school grades is grade inflation, which can be defined as an increase in students' grades without an accompanying increase in their academic achievement. An important difference between grade inflation and other factors influencing the reliability of grades is that grade inflation is an increase in grades over time for students who are at the same level of achievement, while other factors affecting variability in grades result

in assignment of different grades to students at the same level of achievement during the same time period. Because of this, grade inflation is not easy to detect. It requires both examination of grades across time and a stable measure against which to compare them.

Detecting the presence of grade inflation can be accomplished by comparing high school grades to an objective measure of student achievement that is stable over time: the ACT Composite score is such a measure. Examining results over a thirteen-year period (1991 to 2003), grade inflation was evident at every Composite score point and the report concluded that "it may be more accurate to conclude that high school grades have inflated 12.5 percent between 1991 and 2003."

Subsequent to this study, Goodwin (2011) reports on two additional large-scale studies across the United States:

1. Nearly twice as many high school students reported earning an *A* or *A-* average in 2006 than in 1992 (32.8 percent versus 18.3 percent).
2. In 2007, two federal reports found that the performance of U.S. high school students on the reading portion of the National Assessment of Educational Progress (NAEP) had declined between 1992 and 2005, even though students reported getting higher grades (GPAs rose from 2.68 in 1990 to 2.98 in 2005) and taking tougher classes (the percentage of students who said they took college-preparatory classes rose from 5 to 10 percent).

Personal experience reveals how difficult it is to bring this information to the attention of politicians. Their reluctance to acknowledge the problem suggests fearfulness that raising this issue in the public forum will anger teachers and cost votes. It is easier to trade fairness to students, who cannot vote, than expose a significant issue undermining the credibility of the nation's school system.

Some of these reluctant politicians are required to also affix their signatures to students' transcripts. Once they become aware of how inconsistent teacher-generated marks can be, these signatories become complicit in this fraudulent process, and they should be challenged for their willingness to disadvantage some students for the benefit of less deserving ones. Maya Angelou said, "Courage is the most important of all the virtues because without courage, you can't practice any other virtue consistently." Providing students with a free education is now accepted, while providing this in a fair manner requires courage.

It is worthwhile at this point to reiterate the lack of research demonstrating that teachers' class marks are consistent from teacher to teacher. This chapter provides details regarding this unfairness to students from studies in many places. Grade inflation is endemic worldwide. Public naivety regarding this problem of inconsistent assessment is at the crux of many issues percolating in the education system. Consistent student assessment is a fallacy leading to fraudulent results.

It may be difficult for some Americans to appreciate the "hand in glove" metaphor related to Common Core and common assessment. Approximately half of the states use exit examinations; however, an analysis similar to the information recorded above is missing. The interconnectedness of these studies on grade inflation within the educational system demonstrates the concern regarding fairness to students seeking entry into post-secondary institutions. A student should qualify for scholarships and gain entry to prestigious universities because of *merit based on achievement rather than luck based on location of residence or to which teacher they were assigned.*

GRADE INFLATION LEADS TO LOWER LEVELS OF STUDENT ACHIEVEMENT

Disadvantaging worthy students is not the only unfairness that results from grade inflation, as Thomas and Bainbridge's earlier referenced study points out. They found in their study of six schools that students who received high grade point averages had lower scores on the SAT and standardized tests. Where grade inflation was the greatest, actual student achievement as measured by standardized assessments was the lowest.

Laurie (2007) undertook a similar study in Canada's Maritime Provinces located across the U.S. border north of New England. His finding, subsequently replicated in my regional research, found that in schools where students received marks most above their Diploma Examination scores, the examination scores were relatively the lowest in the test group. The opposite was also true: in schools where students experienced the least grade inflation they had the relatively highest examination scores.

Students who receive inflated marks from their schools do not demonstrate similarly high levels of achievement on exit examinations because *they suffer from a false sense of security*. They mistakenly believe they are doing well in the course. Schools that expect little and provide high grades, regardless of the level of academic achievement, are *purveyors of a fraudulent education* that leaves parents and children believing something that is not true. Such action is unconscionable and should be exposed, confronted, and corrected.

One superintendent expressed her difficulty in adequately responding to a group of graduating students, who had received high marks from their school but significantly lower marks on their final examination. The university had advised these students who had been provisionally accepted that they were rejected because the combined score from the exam and the teacher was too low. Dreams were shattered and the superintendent—the visible scapegoat—became the object of an outpouring of anger.

This pattern of grade inflation was evident year after year for many students in the same class. Students were lulled into apathy, or, even worse, into visions of self-aggrandizement, by thinking they had "aced the course"; consequently, they were not diligent about preparing. In this specific instance, the superintendent had the uncomfortable task of saying that nothing could be done except for them to retake the course next year.

This unfortunate incident illustrates the general inability of teachers to grade student achievement in an objective and accurate manner. Webber et al. (2009) summarized their interviews with secondary school principals by stating that "secondary principals were not very positive about teacher knowledge and practice in matters of fairness and equity and assessment." Yet stakes are high in secondary schools where scholarships are won and entrances to prestigious universities are granted.

TEACHERS GRADUATE FROM A SYSTEM
PLAGUED BY GRADE INFLATION

Educators may excuse this tendency to inflate grades by pointing out that grade inflation is rampant in universities as well. Teachers come out of an education system where marks below "B" seldom occur and failure is virtually non-existent. Koedel (2011) analyzed major academic depart-

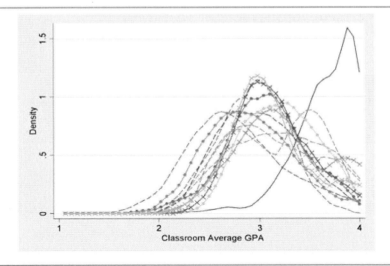

Figure 6.3.

ments at several American universities and reported how education marks are skewed upward (see figure 6.3). Grade point averages for students enrolled in the department of education were much higher than they were in any other department.

Koedel found that

> students who take education classes at universities receive significantly higher grades than students who take classes in every other academic discipline. The higher grades cannot be explained by observable differences in student quality between education majors and other students, nor can they be explained by the fact that education classes are typically smaller than classes in other academic departments. The remaining reasonable explanation is that the higher grades in education classes are the result of low grading standards. These low grading standards likely will negatively affect the accumulation of skills for prospective teachers during university training. More generally, they contribute to a larger culture of low standards for educators. . . . While all other university departments work in one space, education departments work in another. . . . The data consistently show that education departments award exceptionally favorable grades to virtually all their students in all their classes.

Babcock (2010) indicates that *grade inflation is associated with reduced student effort* in college: put simply, students in classes where it is easier to get an "A" do not work as hard. He demonstrated that in classes where the expected *grade point average* rises by one point, students respond by reducing effort, as measured by study time, by at least 20 percent. The implication for education, therefore, is that *teachers who are being trained know less because their marks are so high.*

Using the data from figure 6.3, Koedel estimates, "If the grading standards in each education department were moved to align with the average grading standards at their respective universities, *student effort would rise by at least 11–14 percent.*" Koedel provides a hypothesis regarding why education departments having these deplorably skewed results escape detection.

> One notable difference between education departments and other major departments at universities is that virtually all graduates from education departments move into a single sector of the labor market—education. If the education sector is less effective at identifying low-quality graduates than are other sectors of the labor market, this would help explain why professors in education departments are able to consistently award As to most students.

Most university departments serve a diverse market. For example, the business department seeks to place graduates in an array of firms who can easily discern the differences in the quality of graduates from another institution. *Firms would cease hiring from lower-quality programs, forcing instructors to recalibrate their standards.* Education, on the other hand, is a closed system. Graduates are generally employed locally by the school board, which participates in fostering a culture of low standards. Like the university's department of education, the local school district is reluctant to distinguish good teachers from mediocre teachers.

We have also pointed out that accountability in post-secondary education is out of balance and skewed because it relies on student satisfaction surveys. Over time, academic grades for work of comparable quality have increased in what is known as the "standards creep." It appears that the faculties of education also suffer from a severe case of having low expectations for their students who, eventually, work with our children preparing them for the real world.

GRADE INFLATION IS HIGHEST FOR THE HIGHER ACHIEVERS

Wall (2003) proposes another reason for rampant grade inflation following her investigation, which concluded that "grade inflation is prominent in most schools today. Perhaps it is due to the emphasis on morale. It could also be due to the emphasis of having good grades in order to get into good colleges and become successful." Wall's research and conclusion is generalizable throughout the literature but begs the question as to *why it occurs in elementary and middle school as well.* Students at these grade levels do not need a "leg up" to gain entry into some prestigious university program.

In my regional study, students wrote system-wide tests in grades 3, 6, and 9. These were low-stakes tests, and teachers were encouraged to mark their students' written responses as a first read or as a preliminary reading before the school forwarded the tests to a marking center where anonymity was ensured. This process enabled the school system to study the impact a teacher-student relationship had on the grade a student received. Specifically, the student's teacher and an anonymous teacher marked the same piece of work, and we could determine whether there were differences and, if so, what the trend might be.

The first phase of this study took five years and demonstrated a consistent result for each year and at each grade of the tests. At the Acceptable Standard, up to 8 percent more students achieved a "pass" from their classroom teacher than from the anonymous marker. At the Standard of Excellence, 86 percent more students received an "A"-level mark from their classroom teacher than from the anonymous marker. Because *grade inflation in the classroom was so dramatic at the upper achievement levels,* a meeting with superintendents was held to discuss the problem.

Superintendents were loath to undertake any action to ameliorate the problem. Large-scale testing was contentious and acknowledging these significantly different results in marks was thought to be inflammatory and likely lead to a backlash from union members, which included principals. In the five years that followed, 79 percent more students still received the Standard of Excellence mark from their classroom teacher than from the marking center where student anonymity was tightly controlled. *Teachers' inconsistent marking is a problem made more worrisome by their tendency to inflate student scores, especially scores at the upper levels.*

Unfortunately, grade inflation, which unfairly disadvantages and advantages students, is not the only malevolent feature at work in the marking process. Subjectivity can seriously distort academic achievement as the Pan-Canadian Assessment Program (PCAP) demonstrates. This program includes extensive surveying that provides a context in which we can assess the nature of various relationships associated with student achievement.

One question asked teachers whether they incorporate *improvement* over a period of time when they assigned letter grades related to achievement. In other words, were students' final marks on how well they could divide influenced by how much they improved from the beginning of the term? Teachers who responded affirmatively in the different provinces ranged from 13 percent to 72 percent. A second year, but with a different subject and different teachers responding to the same question, indicated a range of 13 percent to 66 percent. These variations demonstrate how assessments of student achievement vary across regions; yet they are consistent across teaching regardless of subject.

Another question focused on *attendance* and asked whether students' marks were influenced by this issue. Presumably students were penalized with lower marks if they were absent for an inordinate number of days. On this issue, teachers from various jurisdictions varied in their responses, ranging from 6 percent to 66 percent. As with the previous question, these high and low responses were not significant outliers. In other words, other jurisdictions were spread out across the range, with several relatively near both ends of the scale.

Teachers also indicated whether their assessment of the student was influenced by his or her *participation* during class activities. Participation is a desired student behavior, but is it indicative of student learning in curriculum outcomes? Once again teachers varied widely in their attitudes, with as few as 12 percent saying they would be influenced in some districts and as many as 63 percent saying they would be in others.

Improvement over time, attendance, and participation are all qualities associated with being a good student. Parents want to know how their child is doing in these areas because they are good predictors of how well their child will perform in the workplace. However, should these qualities be conflated into an index of "good student" when the grade is intended to measure *competency* in a skill or mastery of a concept? Logic suggests that it would be more truthful and more helpful if these valuable qualities were assessed independently and reported elsewhere.

The confusion on this issue opens the door to inconsistency in assessment and, therefore, unfairness toward a segment of the student population. If these or any other criteria (such as behavior, status in the class, cleanliness, or neatness) are considered when reporting achievement in a subject, teacher bias is introduced.

INCORPORATING NON-ACADEMIC FACTORS INTO ACHIEVEMENT REDUCES SUCCESS

For these non-academic factors, it is noteworthy that Alberta was at the lowest end of the scale for all ten provinces on three of the questions surveyed (including the two years when improvement was the focus) and within 3 percent from the bottom on the fourth. Yet this province persistently recorded the *lowest percentage of teacher assessments* for Canadian students with a mark of 70 percent or higher. In other words, *Alberta students had the lowest set of class marks from teachers across the entire country, while having the lowest percentage of teachers conflating marks for learning with behavior.*

At the same time, this province repeatedly scored the *highest across the nation* on national and international assessments. Indeed, in 2003, it scored the highest in the world. *The applicable generalization is that the jurisdiction with the strictest adherence to marking relative to standards, and the least likelihood of subjectivity leading to bias and grade inflation, also had the highest levels of student achievement as measured on standardized tests.*

In 2007, a report from the Council of Ministers of Education, Canada (CMEC) assessed the impact of the teacher commingling attendance, participation, effort, improvement, and behavior with the students' scores in reading achievement. Figure 6.4 demonstrates that on each criterion, students' test marks were significantly lower when the teacher included consideration of the criterion then when it was not considered.

For example, students who had teachers who indicated they did not include *attendance* in their students' marks scored an average of 495 in their reading achievement test. Students who had teachers who indicated they did include *attendance* scored some thirty points lower on the achievement test. In each instance, using a non-academic factor yielded a lower result in this national assessment of reading.

Mean Reading Scores by Use of Specific Non-Academic Criteria for Grading (PCAP- 2007)

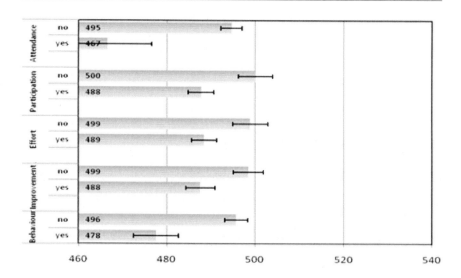

Figure 6.4.

It is apparent, therefore, that teachers who are prone to incorporating non-academic criteria do their students a disservice because including these biases leave students with an inflated understanding of their learning. They experience a disincentive to work harder. In simple language, teachers are disadvantaging their students by not confining their marks to what their students learned.

While Alberta's students benefitted from assessment based on standards, this benefit evaporated when the province's school boards began importing many teachers from the rest of Canada to accommodate a class-size reduction program and the retirement of a significant number of teachers. The national testing program's survey registered an immediate change in the degree to which Alberta teachers utilized *non-academic factors* in assigning final marks for their students.

Previous national studies routinely demonstrated that Alberta teachers were relatively averse to using non-academic factors; with the influx of new teachers, the scores ballooned to the point that 64 percent of Alberta's teachers indicated they were now employing such an approach to grading.

Webber et al. (2009) conducted a follow-up study in Alberta and determined that teachers always or often used factors such as:

- penalties for late assignments (33%)
- adjusted grades to recognize student behavior (17%)
- adjusted grades to recognize neatness (11%)
- adjusted grades based on student attendance (6%)
- bonus marks for extra work (35%)

This study went on to ask students whether they felt teachers assessed a variety of factors in addition to academic achievement when they were given a score in a subject. The results affirmed that this was the case. In their mind, grades were adjusted for the following reasons:

- report card marks change because of late assignments (87% agreed)
- adjust grades to recognize student behavior (47% of secondary and 70% of elementary agreed)
- adjust grades because of how neat the work is (31% at secondary and 69% at elementary agreed)
- bonus marks for extra work (48% agreed)

A summative statement from the researchers indicated that "secondary students admonished that the system is for teachers, not students and *that teacher bias is a real problem.* Students who are favored get better marks. . . . Grades are reduced for misbehavior and if a student is disruptive then grades go down."

Concurrently, a significant shift occurred in the system-wide diploma examination marks. We have already indicated that these examination marks are always lower than school-generated marks. So predictable is this outcome that only rarely do any of the sixty-two school districts record an average examination mark that is higher than that assigned by teachers. Despite the province's outstanding success on the world stage of international testing, there still was grade inflation, albeit to a lesser degree than in any other Canadian jurisdiction.

During a three-year period of extensive teacher hiring and turnover, grade inflation increased dramatically. At the beginning of this three-year period, only *three* districts had a variance greater than 10 percent between the average school and examination marks for English. Three years later, *seventeen* districts *exceeded* the 10 percent threshold; this occurred even though provincial examination marks demonstrated a *significant decline.*

In mathematics, this threshold was *exceeded* by only *five* districts at the beginning of the study but increased to *eighteen* by the conclusion of Webber et al.'s study. The significant increase in school-generated marks was not matched by a similar gain in learning on the provincial exit examination. In the initial year of this study, 83 percent of students met the examination's Acceptable Standard; three years later it remained essentially the same (82 percent).

The same was true with the highest level, known as the Standard of Excellence: over the three year period the decline was inconsequential. Since these exams are now set to be equal in difficulty from year to year, all that changed was the teacher-generated mark, which increased significantly and reflected a new interpretation of the standards.

During this time period another disturbing story emerged from surveys of employers conducted by the province. Their satisfaction with graduates' skills and quality of work plummeted to their lowest level, with a decline from 77 percent satisfaction to 67 percent. Such a dramatic decline had never occurred before, which raised concerns about a growing mismatch between teachers' ability to assess students' achievement and employers' need to have skilled workers. This variation between classroom marks and employer perceptions provided another indication that grade inflation within the classroom was increasing.

Introducing non-academic factors into the assessments of student achievement produced significant grade inflation at a time when national and international assessments indicated achievement was actually declining. Meanwhile, class size reduction, which was purported to improve the learning environment, required the province to increase the number of teachers by 13 percent. Growth in enrollment and a wave of retirements associated with an aging workforce also drove up the number of hires, many of whom were unfamiliar with the province's curricular standards. These factors coalesced to create a negative impact on achievement.

A SIMPLE ILLUSTRATION OF HOW
GRADE INFLATION OCCURS

One more point needs to be made. The longitudinal data reveals how insidious grade inflation can be. Both the examination and school marks were based on percentages, and school marks were skewed significantly to the right. Because student test scores produced a normal distribution, we can be confident that test developers successfully differentiated students on the basis of achievement.

School-generated marks, however, did not demonstrate a normal distribution, which meant factors other than student achievement were in play. For example, in one course required for university entrance, more than three times as many students received a mark of 80 percent than those recorded in the examination. At 90 percent it was double, and school marks were significantly skewed upward beginning at 70 percent. There was another curious fact that strongly suggested the presence of human bias and predilection.

In our modern economy we often "round up" or "down" in an effort to make things simpler. In teacher-recorded marks, the study revealed a very discernible pattern of rounding up that had nothing to do with achievement. For example, there were many scores that ended in zeroes or fives—far more than would have been statistically expected. At the same time, there were disproportionately few grades recorded as either X8 or X9.

Schools were systematically *bumping up marks* by one or two percentage points to qualify for a higher letter grade or scholarship. The rounding up was not compensated for with a corresponding rounding down, and while this explains a minor portion of how grade inflation occurs, the story does not end here. Because the bump ups were not universally applied, so that fewer students received a mark ending in 8 or 9, we can assume that some teachers and some schools took a different approach to assessment. In other words, some teachers did not round up marks for students ending in X8 or X9.

Students in the rounding up schools temporarily benefited, but others did not. To what do we attribute this fundamental unfairness? Gender? Compliant behavior? This question will be discussed, in part, later. The point here is that a pattern of unfairness exists in the system and the evidence extends across all subjects and over many years. Application of certain biases was routinely practiced at the school level and contributed to the natural inclination toward grade inflation. Lower standards at the school level were the norm.

STUDENT CHEATING AND GRADE INFLATION

It is possible that concerns with grade inflation at the school level are compounded by a disconcerting problem that is frequently overlooked and often not even acknowledged. Cheating can profoundly inflate a student's grade, but it could be essentially eliminated on achievement tests if the school followed prescribed protocols. Perhaps this issue is too disconcerting for educators to even acknowledge. If factual, student cheating can seriously jeopardize student fairness.

Academic cheating in post-secondary institutions is well documented. This is less so for the K–12 system, although what we do know is equally disturbing. McCabe et al. (2001) studied high school cheating involving 4,500 U.S. schools and found that:

- 74% of students admitted to serious test cheating
- 72% admitted to serious cheating on written work
- 97% admitted to copying homework or to test copying
- 30% admitted to repetitive, serious cheating on tests/exams
- 15% had obtained a term paper from the Internet
- 52% had copied a few sentences from a website without citing the source

Unfortunately, the *2002 Report Card on the Ethics of American Youth* determined that cheating was *on the rise*. Comparing their student survey results for 1992 and 2002, the percentage of students admitting that they had cheated on an examination increased from 61 percent to 74 percent.

Newberger (1999) compared data with that from the 1940s and found that in a 1997 survey of high achievers in high school, 87 percent judged cheating to be "common" among their peers. Seventy-six percent confessed that they themselves had cheated. By way of contrast, a national sample of U.S. college students in the 1940s found that only 20 percent admitted to cheating in high school when they were questioned anonymously. Cheating is considerably more prevalent today, and, contrary to some people's beliefs, *cheating is not restricted to weak students attempting to improve their chances at passing.*

Niels (2014) researched the major reasons why students cheat and published his results online on the website About.com (January 17, 2014). His research led him to believe that students cheated for the following reasons:

1. There is a mechanism within each of us that triggers a need to "save face." Saving face can mean a desire to save oneself from the angry assault of a parent or teacher.
2. Cheating is no longer deviant behavior because everybody does it.
3. Cheating offers an easy way out. Why bother studying hard and doing all those term papers by yourself if you can use someone else's work?

Niels's findings support the notion that cheating can occur with students of *every ability level whenever they see the need to get ahead without expending the necessary effort*. These findings also imply that the odds of being caught are relatively small.

Newberger (1999) also verifies that the odds of getting away with academic cheating are heavily in the cheater's favor: "Ninety per cent of the confessed cheaters surveyed by *Who's Who* said they had never been caught. . . . The incentive has changed from passing by the weak student to getting into select universities by the stronger students."

In my regional study, cheating on standardized, system-wide tests, where the process occurs under tight security, was very low, with an incidence rate of 1 percent whenever two or more students were detected as having the same pattern of answers. Invigilators systematically monitored the examination room; furthermore, students writing the same test were surrounded with open space and could be observed from multiple angles.

It is noteworthy that in the few instances when students did cheat, *they were writing tests they deemed to be of the greatest importance*. This included, in particular, tests in subjects that were required for a graduation diploma and entrance into university. In other words, these students were the stronger ones wishing to retain their place in the system, who would eventually gain entry into prestigious university programs and a future well-paying job.

The reality of stronger students cheating in order to succeed in a competitive environment was corroborated by Davis et al. (2009):

> It's not the dumb kids who cheat . . . it's the kids with a 4.6 grade point average who are under such pressure to keep their grades up and get into the best colleges. They're the ones who figure out how to cheat without getting caught. . . . Grades are a commodity in our knowledge society and, with many students, they represent the end goal of schooling.

The goal of "saving face" in an environment that increasingly appears to view cheating as normal is observable in the lower grades. Bushway and Nash (1977) indicated that "academic dishonesty is endemic in all levels of education. In the United States, studies show that 20 percent of students started cheating in the first grade. Similarly, other U.S. studies reveal that 56 percent of middle school students admit to cheating (Decoo 2002).

Canadian researchers have not given as much attention to cheating as those in the United States. Nevertheless, the work that has been done reveals a pattern similar to that found in the United States. In 2006, the Universities of Guelph and Rutgers surveyed fifteen thousand students and found that "73 percent of university students reported instances of serious cheating on written work while in high school."

The discussion on cheating has focused, thus far, on student behavior that is considered covert. There also is an overt form that may not be referred to as cheating because it is an encouraged activity. Davis et al. (2009) describe this activity, which ends up giving some students an advantage over their peers: "Think of a student who receives 'help' from his parents on his science project or her essay. If a student is transparent about the assistance received, she might not receive as high a grade than if the teacher thinks the student did her assignment on her own." How frequently does this type of advantage occur?

The PCAP national testing program asked thirteen-year-old students across the nation how frequently they worked with parents on their homework. Two out of three students affirmed that they received assistance: 35 percent said it occurred a few times a month, 26 percent a few times a week, and 6 percent indicated that it happened almost daily. We likely experience some inner turmoil with any suggestion that this parental assistance is cheating; yet, if the teacher is not aware of it and is assessing the product in any way, some students are advantaged. Some are then disadvantaged. *Unfairness has occurred.*

These surveys also asked teachers to identify how frequently homework assignments were used in determining marks? Given that 44 percent indicated that assignments were used to determine the final mark, it is apparent that some students were clearly advantaged and that the advantage was a significant factor. Ideally teachers are sufficiently astute to track the degree to which their students receive assistance. To the degree that this monitoring does not occur, we can assume that grade inflation is translating as unfairness to students. Ryan (1998) references unfairness resulting from plagiarism, which is equally applicable to any unknown assistance:

> Often lost in the discussion of plagiarism is the interest of the students who don't cheat. They do legitimate research and write their own papers. They work harder (and learn more) than the plagiarists, yet their grades may suffer when their papers are judged and graded against papers that are superior but stolen material. Students have a right to expect fairness in the classroom. When teachers turn a blind eye to plagiarism, it undermines that right and denigrates grades, degrees, and even institutions.

Many teachers and administrators understand how grade inflation occurs because they receive students into their programs who struggle to learn, yet receive relatively high grades. Research evidence indicates that assessment of student achievement is inconsistent because various forms of bias find their way into a teacher's mindset. As offensive as the term "unfairness to students" might seem to some, anytime students are advantaged or disadvantaged by these biases, the result is unfair to some or all. There is no merit in attempting to cloak the issue in secrecy, as so frequently occurs.

The focus in this chapter is about a necessity for linking Common Core with common assessment. Requiring teachers across the participating states to teach to high standards without attaching accountability for ensuring that the standards are taught is inadequate leadership. Teachers want parents and the public to trust unquestioningly their assessments of student learning. Their unions understand that without large-scale testing the entire accountability effort in the K–12 system is at risk—indeed, it collapses. Such an environment is similar to what exists in most postsecondary programs where instructors use "academic freedom" to avoid accountability.

Sole discretion to determine the curriculum and the assessment of learning is the preferred situation for teachers' unions, which argue that every learning environment is unique and therefore nothing is in common and capable of standardization. This leaves the classroom an impregnable fortress in which the teacher, the lord of the domain, rules benevolently without fear of accountability.

It is a scenario that cannot and will not survive. Public scrutiny today, born in part out of a growing awareness of the conclusions researchers are drawing from multiple longitudinal studies, makes it clear that the old way must go. Trust will remain, but in a new and open context in which respectful dialogue and a new attitude of cliental service emerges.

The global community is altering the K–12 system because the advent of standardized testing now identifies which countries are providing higher levels of student learning. Results from these cyclical tests are like the sports environment where athletes come together every four years for athletic contests. In education, these tests are like an "Olympics of Learning," but with one significant variation: Rather than involving the elite athletes, as in sports, random samples of the general student population are involved in measuring education. The focus, therefore, is on the average.

As in sport, where countries undertake initiatives to improve athletic performance, and thereby raise the bar of excellence for themselves and others, educational leaders today also feel pressure to stay abreast of rising international standards. Strategies for improvement may be in the form of increased resources or accountability. The result is that politics more than ever before are involved with education and, when this occurs, politicians inevitably choose sides.

The message of this chapter is that fairness to students requires a check-and-balance approach that features large-scale testing of student achievement in regard to common standards. The results leave students and their parents with an ability to judge for themselves how well the student is learning and to be confident that the measurement is a fair and accurate assessment of what it purports to measure.

This, in turn, creates the possibility of holding accountable those who are responsible for the learning environment. It is this measurement process that applies pressure on those within the educational system to improve their performance. *Reaction against this pressure is what produces the increasing opposition to Common Core among Democrats.*

Teachers' unions need to reexamine their resistance to large-scale testing. The evidence of the teacher's inability to assess student achievement in a consistent and fair manner is overwhelming. In an effort to be fair to students, unions must become advocates of a new approach that puts the best interests of students first while trusting that the welfare of teachers will be appropriately addressed. *As it now stands, unions are the significant inhibitors of fairness to students.*

Politicians faced with this conflict have to consider their potential to win the next electoral contest. Will they side with the unions, which can readily influence their members' votes? Will they side with students, who have limited understanding of fairness issues and cannot vote? To what extent will they release information to the public so that they are more informed about the nature of the conflict? These are significant issues in educational politics, and it is necessary to draw politicians into the discussion so that their positions are clearly stated and publicly understood.

While we trust our service providers it is folly to do it so blindly. As Edward Deming once stated, "In God we trust, all others bring data." The data story in student assessment should provide our elected representatives with the evidence they need to take a public, persuasive stand that makes fairness to students the highest priority in their education platform.

The key points made in this chapter are as follows:

- Common Core introduces high standards for all America's students.
- Common assessment is a tipping point in the matter of blind trust in educators versus fairness to students.
- Common Core is easily undone if common assessment is not evident.
- Research verifies that teachers' marks are a very unreliable means of measurement.
- Teachers find it relatively easy to place students' papers in a rank order from best to poorest but find it difficult to rate them against standards.
- Students are winners or losers because of their teachers' specific biases.
- Conspicuous by its absence in educational research is evidence that there is consistency in assessment.
- Inconsistency in assessment is the central issue, but it is exacerbated by a tendency toward grade inflation.
- Most people in the public do not understand that any test given to one or more students is a standardized test.
- Grade inflation is a serious problem because it is fraudulent.
- Grade inflation leads to lower levels of student achievement.

- Teachers are naturally inclined toward grade inflation because they graduate from a system plagued by grade inflation.
- Grade inflation is highest for the higher achievers.
- Incorporating non-academic factors into achievement reduces success.
- Grade inflation can be the result of student cheating reported to be rampant in schools.

SEVEN

Teacher Gender and Fairness to Boys

Chapter 6 demonstrated how students can be advantaged or disadvantaged by teachers' inconsistent assessments. Marks are a student's currency for accessing scholarships and educational programs, and unfairness to students occurs when biases are introduced into their assessments. Unfairness may result in unearned high marks, which provide a false sense of security, or undeserved lower marks, which prevent future success.

Focusing on inconsistency is uncomfortable to educators because human fallibility is not easy to overcome, and the degree to which this is true provides credence for the need to incorporate standardized testing coupled with anonymous marking. Much of the debate regarding standardized tests revolves around the issues of comparability and consistency. The former is associated with fairness in level of service, whereas the latter deals with fairness in assessment.

The important point in the previous chapter is that teachers' marks are not only inconsistent but also inconsistent in one direction. Inflated grades from classroom teachers are a serious problem in our school system and will continue to plague fairness to students unless the Common Core standards are applied. Bringing this problem to people's attention may disturb our educational environment where political correctness is so dominant; however, most people, including politicians, are oblivious to the extent that grade inflation occurs. The value that standardized testing has in providing consistent assessment cannot be overstated.

This chapter adds another dimension to the problem of fairness for students. Specifically, is fairness compromised by gender? In other words, is student success related to the gender of the student while in school? Does the data demonstrate trends that place one gender *at risk for fairness*?

GRADE INFLATION'S GENDER ADVANTAGE

The problem of grade inflation begs the question regarding whether every student has an inflated mark or only some students? Douglas Reeves, an American expert on assessment, provided an insightful exchange of e-mails when he stated that "teacher bias that I have observed is most insidious not in the tests themselves, but in the *conflation of academic performance and behavior* when translating test performance into marks for the report card." If behavior influences student letter grades, are there some whose behavior advantages them more than others?

If there is a discernible pattern that demonstrates a bias, then the issue of fairness rears its ugly head. As Reeves explains,

> Students (disproportionately minority girls in my research) receive higher letter grades for lower actual achievement, because of their quiet, compliant and respectful attitude. I will note, parenthetically, that I'm all in favor of quiet, compliant and respectful behavior among teenagers—I just wish that we would not call these characteristics "algebra" or "physics."

Webber et al. (2009) similarly concluded that culture influenced student marks, stating that "almost 60 percent of educators perceived that students' cultural background affected the grades these students got."

Reeves explains further how the bias serves to disadvantage male students, and adds the observation that teachers readily discern a dichotomy between test and class marks:

> Other students (disproportionately boys) receive lower letter grades for higher actual achievement, because of disorganization and oppositional behavior. Every time I ask teachers if they can think of students who make A's and B's on tests yet receive D's or F's in the class, almost every hand goes up.

Harlen (2004), synthesizing twenty-three studies from the United Kingdom and the United States, also concluded that evidence of gender bias exists by stating that "teachers'" judgments of the academic performance of young children are *influenced by the teachers' assessment of their behavior*; this adversely *affects the assessment of boys compared with girls."* Kathryn Scantelbury (2009) put it somewhat differently: "Overall, teachers have *lower expectations* for girls' academic success compared to boys."

Webber et al. (2009), after surveying and interviewing teachers, found that a surprisingly high percentage of teachers actually acknowledged a gender bias:

> Almost 1 in 4 (23%) of educators agree "students' gender" affects the grades they get. However, qualitative data suggests that frequently gender was linked with behavior in that boys were perceived to be more likely to be disruptive and less compliant, which in turn influenced the grades that teachers assigned to boys.

In other words, while only one in four teachers *openly* acknowledged gender bias, the interview process revealed the potential for boys to be disadvantaged when having their work assessed because of their *lower levels of compliant behavior.*

It is discouraging to think that biases based on gender could find a way into our school system. We expect fairness and consistency to be foundational in our society; yet *we don't expect it to occur in our classrooms.* Some stakeholders may feel defensive about this unacceptable situation, and so the regional study delved into this issue at considerable length by assessing gender bias for students from grade 1 through to university.

In regional mathematics tests, male students scored higher on grades 3, 6, and 9 system tests at both the Acceptable Standard and the Standard of Excellence. When teachers were required to report their assessment of each student's achievement on the report card, more males in grades 1–9 were assessed as functioning *below grade level in every grade.* In these grades, students' final marks were based exclusively on the teachers' assessment because the system tests were given in the final week of the school year after report cards were already completed.

At the end of grade 9, students self-selected a mathematics stream for senior high school that would lead to university programing. Unfortunately for male students, programing decisions are made in April for the following September. Since system tests occur at the end of June, classroom marks weigh heavily in decisions. Students and their parents did not receive their grade 9 system test results until the end of September, well after they had begun their grade 10 course. Participation rates in the grade 10, upper-stream mathematics course favored females even though males demonstrated higher proficiency on the system tests.

This aspect of the study is significant because grade 10 programing is the first screen in choosing a career. Enrolling in the lower-stream mathematics course curtails qualification for university acceptance and, coincidentally, career aspirations. Mathematics is a significant gate-keeper into the world of work, and the screening process, influenced by the biases as are presented, is eliminating many males from contending.

Experiencing a disadvantage in *gaining placement* in the upper-stream mathematics course, male students continue to experience a negative bias, further limiting their potential for scholarships and acceptance by universities. In this study, school-awarded marks and examination marks each count for 50 percent of the final course mark, and more female students received the Standard of Excellence from the *school awarded marks* while more males received this high standard on the Diploma Examination. This pattern of assessment was consistent over a period of seven consecutive semesters.

From a broader perspective of examining all courses in English, mathematics, sciences, and social studies, the analysis underscores an advantage for female students. Aggregating seven consecutive semesters across these courses—seventy tests—females received *almost double* the "A" marks received by males from teachers' *class marks*—that is, 13.3 percent of females received "A's" while 6.7 percent of males received "A's." *Diploma Examination marks* told a different story, as females received only 7 percent more "A" marks. This 14:1 ratio provides females with a significant advantage when calculating final marks and qualifying for scholarships and placements in post-secondary education.

Considering only the *upper-stream courses*, which are critical determinants for accessing universities, school-level "A" marks were 66 percent more frequent than diploma examination "A" marks, which demonstrates the high level of grade inflation for these important subjects. *Classroom* "A" marks favored females by 11.4 percent, while *examination* "A" marks favored males by 8.1 percent. Since the data set demonstrates significant grade inflation at the school level, females receive substantial advantage in securing scholarships and placements into prestigious universities.

The point in this data is that far more teachers assess students' work in their classrooms at the "A" level than are scored anonymously on regional tests. A second point pertains to the distribution of these "A" marks, where female students are more likely to receive an "A" from their teacher who is knowledgeable about the test writers' gender.

A superintendent, who became aware of these disturbing trends, undertook a study in his school district. He tracked all student marks by gender as they progressed through high school, monitoring trends as students went from one teacher gender to the other. His review revealed a disturbing fact.

Female students going from a grade where the teacher was a female to a grade where the teacher was a male experienced a *bump up* in their marks. While males progressing from a male to a female teacher also benefited, the bump up was not significant. When the superintendent apprised his principals with these findings, he was greatly disturbed by their response: they readily acknowledged the situation and referred to it as the "halter-top effect." This sad revelation underscores how bias can intervene in efforts to ensure fairness for students.

The advantage for female students evident in the regional study also translated into a 2007 *Stats Can* national report for Canada titled "Why Are Most University Students Women":

> The gap in university attendance is largely associated with differences in academic performance and study habits at the age of 15, parental expectations, and other characteristics of men and women. . . . Weaker academic performance among men accounted for almost one-half (45%) of the gap. Specifically, young men had lower overall school marks at age 15 and had poorer performance on a standardized reading test. . . . In the 2001 Census, universities had clearly become the domain of women, as they made up 58 percent of all graduates. . . . We find the differences in the characteristics of boys and girls account for more than three quarters (76.8%) of the gap in university participation. In order of importance, the main factors are differences in school marks at age 15 (31.8%).

The *school mark* is the leading contributor for answering the question of "Why are most university students women?" The message in this study is made more significant when we factor in that most Canadian students progressing from high school to university submit marks only generated by their teachers. In other words, most provinces do not have exit examinations in grade 12 that counterbalance the biased marks from teachers. The "weaker academic performance among men" is a significant factor, given the evidence that demonstrates *their marks are impacted negatively by noncompliant behaviors.*

When the school system does not implement standardized testing accompanied by anonymous marking, the male gender is disadvantaged when seeking entry into universities. York University in Ontario already is reporting its enrollment as 70 percent female, which is significant because Ontario suffers from the highest levels of grade inflation in Canada. *The higher the rate of grade inflation, the greater the chance for female acceptance into universities because of their more compliant school behaviors.*

In the United States, Williams (2010) reports how American women represent about 57 percent of enrollments at American colleges since the year 2000. According to this report, the American Council on Education concludes that, at registration, women tend to have higher grades and their enrollment skews higher among older students, low-income students, and black and Hispanic students.

Borzelleca (2012) writes in *Forbes*:

> On a national scale, public universities had the most even division between male and female students, with a male-female ratio of 43.6–56.4. While that difference is substantial, it still is smaller than private not-for-profit institutions (42.5–57.5) or all private schools (40.7–59.3). The nearly 40–60 ratio of private schools was most surprising, though perhaps this is partly due to the fact that most all-female schools are private. Nevertheless, the female domination of higher education prevails across all types of schools. It should also be noted that the national male-female ratio for 18–24 year olds is actually 51–49, meaning there are more (traditionally) college-aged males than females.

Even though more males are living, a much lower percentage of them are attending university. Part of the reason for such low enrollment for males may be explained in an October 2006 article in the *American School Board Journal*, where the authors suggested what administrators might find when examining their districts:

> Boys, they'll probably notice, make up 80 to 90 percent of the district's discipline referrals, 70 percent of learning disabled children, and at least two-thirds of the children on behavioral medication. They'll probably find that boys earn two-thirds of the Ds and Fs in the district, but less than half the As. On statewide standardized test scores, they'll probably notice boys behind girls in general. They may be shocked to see how far behind the boys are in literacy skills; nationally, the aver-

age is a year and a half. The moment an administrator sees the disparity of achievement between boys and girls can be liberating. Caring about children's education can now include caring about boys and girls specifically.

In my regional study, three times as many male students were coded with moderate or severe disabilities, and two times more with mild or moderate disabilities. At the same time, males coded with different types of disabilities generally *tended to outperform* coded females when teachers assessed their grade level of achievement. *In other words, more male students were identified as "special needs" but assessed as demonstrating higher achievement by teachers.* An obvious question is: Should all of these males have been coded, or were they being boys in a female-dominated world? Definitely, *caring about fairness for boys and girls specifically is a transformational issue for education.*

Discussions about gender issues can be contentious, especially when it is implied that one gender is advantaged by human actions. Suggesting that bias is compromising fairness may strike many educators as repugnant and, perhaps, generate a degree of hostility. The point in this chapter is to add to the observation from chapter 6—teachers are prone to inflate student marks—by demonstrating that the inflated marks are not equal across the genders. Female students are the primary beneficiaries.

Treating everyone unfairly can be fair. Treating a segment of the population in a different manner is unfair. Marks are a student's currency for achieving scholarships and acquiring placement in post-secondary education. When bias is evident in the distribution of this currency, the school system is obligated to utilize processes to mitigate unfairness.

Common assessments for all students provide greater accountability in the education system, including a means for countering grade inflation. These standardized tests are not feasible unless there is a common set of standards as provided in the Common Core.

The key points made in this chapter are as follows:

- Grade inflation is not applied equally: females benefit more because of their tendency toward compliant behavior.
- Despite higher achievement on system tests, when teachers were required to report their assessment of each student's achievement on the report card, more males in grades 1–9 were assessed as functioning *below grade level in every grade.*

- Male students are disadvantaged from lower marks impacted by their noncompliant behaviors when streaming into higher-level programming occurs.
- Male students in higher-level programs score well on standardized tests but are disadvantaged when inflated classroom assessments, which favor female students, are incorporated into the overall marks.
- The perceived weaker academic performance of male students significantly explains why universities are predominantly female.

EIGHT

Common Assessment

An Investment

Previous chapters established a pathway beginning with Common Core and how this concept is necessary to provide fairness for students across the nation: at least within those states participating in this initiative. With common standards or expectations in place, the next and necessary step is a program of common assessment so that student success relative to these standards can be measured. *It is not possible to determine whether students receive high-quality instruction without a measurement component being in place.*

Documentation recorded in the previous chapter disturbs our confidence in teachers' capacity to assess student achievement in a manner that is consistent and without bias. This finding, *which is not contradicted within research,* can produce defensive responses from well-intentioned teachers; however, politicians need to deal with this disturbing reality. It is not fair that some deserving students be denied scholarships or placements in prestigious university programs because other students benefit from being in a class where the teacher's marks are inflated to a higher degree.

Assessments of student achievement by standardized tests linked with standards identified in the Common Core are appropriate instruments *especially when accompanied with anonymous marking.* We know that students are less diligent in their studies when they receive inflated marks. Inconsistent officiating in sports is not tolerated, and we should not permit educators to be the sole determinants of student success, either.

Politicians committed to ensuring fairness of educational opportunity as well as in assessing learning to students will achieve their "biggest bang for the buck" when they implement common assessment. Those who fear loss of political support from teachers if common assessment is implemented will not experience the reward of having students in their jurisdictions achieve higher academic success. This chapter will demonstrate the unfortunate reality of supporting the wrong group.

Teachers are supporting Common Core but resisting common assessment. This linkage demonstrates how the proverbial "rubber meets the road" in education. Introducing accountability into the education system has always been contentious, *but more so when student success is measured on an annual basis and it becomes possible to determine their gain scores.* Assigning a value-added component to a teacher's ongoing evaluation provides hard data for assessing the performance of classroom teachers.

ACCOUNTABILITY IS APPLIED UNEQUALLY

Accountability in the public sector is given too little credence. In education it is characterized as an issue with moral implications. Douglas Reeves (2000) stated it eloquently when he said, "As a fundamental moral principle, no child in any school will be more accountable than the adults in the system. Similarly, it is a moral principle of leadership that no teacher or staff member will be more accountable than the leaders in the system."

Subsequent to Reeves's statement about no child being held to greater accountability than his or her teacher, Webber et al. (2009) also conducted a large-scale study on assessment with a similar conclusion; in their minds, "the teacher should be assessed more than the student." These conclusions lead us into an interesting and provocative discussion.

Consider how frequently students are being assessed, and compare this comprehensive schedule to the evaluation program for teachers. Students experience constant informal assessments on a daily basis; yet too many teachers indicate that they seldom are evaluated and that their principal never enters their classroom. Even classroom monitoring is infrequent.

In my region, principals were funded to participate in training for a "classroom walk-through" program, whereby they would enter unannounced for a brief visit lasting but a few minutes. Their participation in this program included training in how to provide teachers with some meaningful feedback that would add value to their teaching. All participants across several school districts committed to *weekly classroom visitations with some feedback on observations for all teachers.*

At the program's conclusion, principals and teachers were surveyed regarding implementation and quality of feedback. Eighty-two percent of eighty-seven school-based administrators indicated that they visited only *three or fewer* classrooms per week. In other words, the principal's visitation program consisted of an average of zero to three classrooms per week.

These schools had many classrooms and most of the teachers surveyed indicated that their classroom was never visited despite the principals' commitment to undertake weekly visits. It is reasonable that many of these principals could be categorized among the enlightened ones, considering the commitment their jurisdictions demonstrated in promoting principal visibility in classrooms. If we were to look at the overall population of school administrators, the percentage of principals being absent from the classroom would be even higher.

This study is a sad commentary on the assessment that is going on in our schools: it is particularly sobering because it reflects poorly on the follow-through of school leaders who committed to an activity and received support through training and special funding. Equally disturbing was the lack of follow through from district administrators who organized their district's participation and provided an advocacy role for this supervision model.

Anecdotal evidence from many teachers indicates how infrequently they ever see their principal in their classroom. Yet students constantly have their work examined because teachers understand the value of monitoring student work and making necessary adjustments to their teaching. *Ongoing monitoring facilitates good coaching, which is a function teachers use with their students, and administrators should be increasing visits with their teachers.*

The point of this anecdote is that students experience frequent formal evaluations while doing their course work. These assessments help to determine their mark, and this process is completed annually throughout their school career. In their "job," accountability for progress and achievement is high. Educators understand that student motivation increases when personal accountability includes frequent feedback and ongoing evaluation.

Commitment to nurturing this motivation in students is actually increasing frequency in evaluations of student learning. America's Race to the Top program incorporates quarterly assessments *of* student learning so that students benefit from more frequent feedback on their success. This increased frequency motivates students and parents by providing them with ongoing information about progress. Teachers benefit by receiving ongoing feedback regarding the degree to which teaching and learning are succeeding.

Contrast this high level of feedback to students with practices employed by those delivering instructional services. Not only do teachers indicate how seldom principals are in their classrooms, but many also indicate that, after receiving their permanent contract, further evaluations are seldom conducted. In America, the EPE Research Center reported in 2008 that only twelve states required annual formal evaluations for teachers. Weisberg et al. (2009) write, "Many teachers—especially more experienced teachers—aren't evaluated every year. These teachers might go years between receiving any meaningful feedback on their performance."

Reeves's moral principle is obviously disregarded. Students have their work inspected and assessed much more frequently than occurs with teachers, and this poor level of teacher supervision is not confined to North America's education system. Jensen and Reichl (2011) report that "Australia's systems of teacher appraisal and feedback are broken, and students are suffering as a result." More specifically,

> No one understands this more than the teachers themselves. 63% of teachers report that appraisals of their work are done purely to meet administrative requirements; 91% say the best teachers do not receive the most recognition and reward; and 71% say that poor-performing teachers in their school will not be dismissed. Instead, assessment and feedback are largely tick-a-box exercises not linked to better classroom teaching, teacher development or improved student results.

When students are evaluated, the focus is on how well they learned the content of their instructional program. Curriculum outcomes are followed in classrooms, and teachers report progress their students make in understanding concepts and mastering skills. While student report cards incorporate elements such as behavior, attendance, and effort, the overwhelming thrust evident in the evaluation is focused on demonstrations of learning relative to curricular outcomes.

Since learning is so important in our culture, it is logical to expect that teacher evaluations will be based on how well their students achieve what is taught. Weisberg et al. (2009) summarize reality, indicating that "student academic progress rarely factors directly into evaluations. Instead, teachers are often evaluated based on superficial judgments about behaviors and practices that may not have any impact on student learning—like the presentation of their bulletin boards." Teacher evaluations are virtually disconnected from their mandate. *Currently, what doesn't seem to matter is what really matters: student achievement.*

When students receive their report cards from teachers they contain vastly different assessment information than what is provided to teachers during their evaluation. A student report card utilizes many categories of learning with *multiple areas of focus*. For example, assessments based on progress in language arts are broken into sub-categories such as reading, listening, spelling, writing, and so on; a similar use of sub-categories is followed within almost all other courses. The point is that students and their parents receive detailed assessments in *multiple areas* of their work.

These assessments are embellished by rating systems that seek to show the degree to which learning and skill development has occurred. The practices of using letter grades (A, B, C, D, and F), percentages, or other coded symbols are fairly common methods for providing *greater precision* in evaluating student achievement. Some teachers even assign "+" or "-" values to letter grades, providing even greater specificity. The point is that student learning is evaluated with a system using *multiple ratings* in *multiple aspects* of a course.

Similar scrutiny and precision is noticeably lacking in teacher evaluations where those doing the assessment typically use a binary approach that rates teachers as "satisfactory" or "unsatisfactory." While "unsatisfactory" is grounds for dismissal, it is rarely used in education. Using "satisfactory" fails to distinguish great teaching from good, and good from fair. The analysis by Weisberg et al. (2009) concluded that "even in districts where evaluations include more than two possible ratings, most teachers earn top marks." *Essentially, teacher evaluations are meaningless because they do not differentiate talent or monitor degrees of success.*

Unlike student reports, where sub-categories of courses are also evaluated, teacher reports seldom, if ever, provide a rating of specific teaching elements. Comments pertaining to these elements may be provided, but an actual proficiency rating seldom occurs. The assessment of the teacher's quality is, in essence, left up to the reader to glean from the written comments. Or, as some school district staff admitted, it is more important in reading teacher evaluation reports to look for what is *not* written. When specific teaching elements are absent in a report, it usually means that there is a weakness that the evaluator chooses not to put into writing.

Up to this point in our comparison between student and teacher accountability, the standard is clearly higher for students. *Reeves's moral principle is being violated*. In fact, the degree to which a double standard is evident is unconscionable. Politicians must be more demanding and teachers' unions more forthcoming. Surely the unions' mandate for teacher welfare can be more than ensuring a job-for-life. Providing feedback to teachers on strengths and weaknesses in a transparent fashion can lead to a more fulfilling career.

The discourse above is focused on confidential reporting. Even though student report cards are written for parents, they still are considered private material. Reporting weak progress publicly would be devastating to a student's self-esteem.

But there is a double standard evident between student and teacher when excellent performance is considered. Students' award ceremonies go well beyond accomplishments in skill-related programs such as sports and the arts. They recognize in many ways and in many venues how well students have achieved academically by providing information about high grade point averages or letter grades. Information regarding scholarships is prominently displayed for public information, and excellence in student achievement is publicly celebrated.

This is not the case for teachers or for excellence in the classroom. Teachers may be celebrated for service outside of the classroom, but recognition based on either their performance evaluations or their success in improving student achievement is not. Yet this is what they are hired to do. Where governments attempt to initiate such recognition, unions move to block the effort. Their unwillingness to recognize excellent teaching is yet another example of the double standard that exists in the education system that is constantly awarding excellence in students.

ADMINISTRATOR ACCOUNTABILITY ALSO FAILS THE TEST

While it is deemed immoral to hold students to a higher level of account-ability than teachers, it is also necessary to hold school administrators to a higher level of accountability than their teachers. Is it possible that administrators do not push for greater teacher accountability because they understand this principle? Are they too immobilized by fear of hav-ing their leadership measured and evaluated?

The wrong-headed issue related to holding students more account-able than their teachers is exacerbated by how principals and superinten-dents are evaluated. For many decades people have articulated the phrase, "what gets measured gets done." This significant statement has been attributed to Peter Drucker, Tom Peters, Edward Deming, Lord Kelvin, and others. Williamson (2006) provides a concise description of measurement:

> As we consider what to measure, we must have a standard or a goal to attain. We must measure current performance as compared to that standard and take intelligent, consistent actions to eliminate problems. But what we measure must be important to both the business and those who directly and indirectly impact what is being measured. Keep in mind when something is measured but it isn't important, it probably won't get done. This speaks to sustainability.

Sustainability in measurement requires that what is measured must be important. This begs the question in education as to what is deemed important. Research studies of more than sixty school board evaluations of their superintendent confirmed how one issue dominated. Specifically, the significant evaluation criterion in these reports was the staff's percep-tion of the superintendent and whether the evaluation was obtained by formal survey or by school board members "dipsticking" their teacher contacts. Superintendents understood that how their leadership was per-ceived by staff was where their "bread was buttered," and they did everything to ensure popularity with their teachers and principals.

Williamson goes on to say, "Measure the wrong things and you will likely get the wrong behaviors. . . . Do the rewards and recognition pro-cesses encourage and reinforce the desired behavior changes?" When recognition systems do not include student achievement, it is unlikely that this area will receive much attention. Hence the resistance to stan-dardized testing for *all students* because the capacity to compare student achievement across schools is too threatening to teachers and principals. Individual efforts by superintendents to implement measures of student achievement become career limiting moves.

What the school boards' evaluations have not ensured is that the superintendent's evaluation is focused on student learning, which is the educational purpose of the system. Focusing on student learning may produce a degree of discomfort. One superintendent pointed out how his suggestion that the school seek ways to improve student learning resulted in immediate pushback. Staff confronted this superintendent with the question "Why aren't you happy with us?" and indicated that the only way they could improve would be if he provided additional funding. This response did not produce happy interactions for the superintendent.

Another superintendent, whom the government's auditor general identified as the most accountable in the state, related his experience when permission was granted that a team of investigators meet with the community for the purpose of identifying best practices for use elsewhere. The auditor general's review team met with the superintendent after their consultations were completed and asked for his opinions. His response focused on perceptions. His relentless emphasis on improving student achievement was not popular in the system and, compared with other superintendents, he was perceived as something of a "sore thumb." His leadership activity stood out as a rebuke to other superintendents.

His single recommendation to the government representatives was that they embrace his focus on student achievement by implementing state accountability initiatives and policies regarding student achievement. He wanted the elected officials to see his approach become the norm, not a disrespected anomaly. Not long after this dialogue with government officials, the state introduced standardized testing as well as a standardized format for school districts when producing annual reports on progress toward publicized goals. Eventually the state also developed report cards on school districts, with a significant focus on student achievement.

The critical point is that common assessment of student achievement potentially alters the dynamics of how educators—teachers and administrators—are evaluated. Assessing the learning of all students each year is a necessary condition in achieving fairness for students. Hard data on student achievement provides the basis for evaluating performance, and this important information motivates service providers to be more diligent while performing what really matters: educating our youth. *Popularity versus performance has a new winner!*

When we make our students highly accountable, we must ensure that our teachers' experience a similar level. If our teachers' experience is analogous, then it follows that their leaders should be similarly held accountable. It then follows that if students, teachers, principals, and superintendents are all held accountable for agreed-upon learning goals, our political leadership must also experience a similar level of accountability.

All levels within the education system must be linked by a set of common purposes and accountability standards. If this does not occur, the centrality of student achievement in the educational system loses preeminence and is lost in the competing agendas of others active in the educational enterprise. It is all about getting "bang for the buck," where the bang is student achievement and well-being and the "buck" is a maximum return on every dollar spent. Meaningless teacher and administrator evaluations can be upgraded significantly by *incorporating common assessments for differentiating talent or monitoring degrees of success.*

The dilemma we face in our governance system is that politicians pander to special interest groups. As already stated, *students are the educational system's customers, not a special interest group.* They can't vote. They don't negotiate contracts that govern how they will be treated or what their rights will be. They don't have a union to protect their rights to fair education. *They are caught with being in the care of people assigned to meet their needs but who have wants of their own that take priority.* Too frequently these wants are in direct competition with the needs of the primary customer: our children and the educational system's students.

This description is not intended to describe their status as persona non grata. There are laws that protect them from various forms of physical abuse. There are policies that prescribe how they will be programmed academically. But education is ambiguous about too many significant issues, and policies are too frequently non-binding. More specifically, there is a long history of disregard for measuring student learning and achievement, and their intellectual and academic needs are too frequently subjugated by the selfish wants of special interest groups.

Reiterating the point, common assessment linked with Common Core alters the prevailing dynamics in education where popularity is more important than performance. The point in this discussion is that common assessment provides trend-line information regarding a teacher's ongoing performance in the classroom and administrator's leadership in our schools. This information is of high value and more credible than the type of performance reviews currently provided.

MOVE AWAY FROM INPUTS TOWARD OUTCOMES

Improvement necessitates a change in perspective. The public is predisposed to measuring inputs where judgments regarding quality are based on the amount of funding invested in programs and services. Governments are to blame for this perspective because their response to any problem in our society generally includes a commitment to throw more money at it. Funding levels are readily measured and compared. Therefore the public is used to the notion that spending more will achieve more. *People frequently confuse activity with effectiveness* because they think that the act of doing something will improve the situation automatically.

Once a program is in place the law of inertia sets in and it continues because it is difficult for political leadership to retreat from commitments, and people in those programs can put government officials on the defensive when they contemplate the elimination of their program. For example, educators can quickly rally a parent group to complain vociferously when a funding cut is projected for a program in which their child is enrolled. People are still persuaded by the subjective anecdotal evidence the educators provide, even though it is recognized that the teachers have a great deal of time invested in the program and their jobs will likely be threatened if the legislators reduce funding.

When a school applies for and receives special funding for a new program, parents are easily persuaded of the program's virtue when their child is identified for placement. Studies reveal that evaluations of these programs lack rigor associated with empirical data based on student outcomes. Rather, qualitative assessments are utilized focusing on attitudes about being in the program. Considerations to remove funding for the program are countered with strong opposition generated by parents with children who receive special attention.

What is always interesting about these instances is that the school or, for that matter, the school district, appears to place little value on the efficacy of these programs. There is excitement in launching a new venture but not in conducting a tedious effort to evaluate the outcomes. Experience has shown that assessments are usually based on survey results focused on qualitative evaluation rather than quantitative. Respondents, typically teachers and parents, are biased because parents like the special attention their child is receiving and teachers like the fact that they can pursue their passion (or else they like that the program has removed a particular problem from their workload).

If it is determined that an initiative truly has value in terms of improving outcomes, it is logical to expect that a school would retain the program and find funding by withdrawing resources from other programs where "bang for the buck" is less. This exchange seldom happens, however. The emotional pain associated with ending a program and deploying those resources toward a more promising venture seems too great.

More broadly speaking, the problem is that governments implement new initiatives resulting in added cost to taxpayers but they seldom evaluate worthiness to determine whether programs should continue. When the next need is determined, they resort, once again, to their predisposition to throw money at problems. *Funding is seldom found from within the system but is merely added, and so the bill to taxpayers keeps increasing.* Soon a smorgasbord of initiatives is operating in the system, which prevents the measurement of any particular program's worthiness.

This can be illustrated by a Canadian provincial government that increased its annual operational funding to the education system by 112 percent over a fourteen-year period. During this same time period, inflation only increased by 47 percent and student population increased by 9 percent. Funding the original set of *needs*—inflation and growth—fourteen years later required an additional 56 percent. Coincidentally, the expansionary budget necessary to fund newly identified *wants* was also 56 percent. During this fourteen-year period, the government added an average of 4 percent annual spending beyond inflation and growth for newly identified initiatives.

These additional expenditures included efforts to decrease class sizes across all grade levels but especially in primary grades. This effort was supplemented by an initiative to improve reading achievement among primary children. Even though these initiatives were focused on children in the primary grades, class sizes in high school courses were reduced considerably.

More funding was allocated for dealing with increased numbers of children identified as possessing mild to moderate disability. This latter increase was ironic because an audit of this category revealed 50 percent of students identified by school personnel did not meet the criterion. Removing the annual audit process resulted in a dramatic increase in the number of students identified as special needs because schools recognized that the government had created a "cash cow" they could milk for all it was worth.

Another significant grant was given to the system for exploring new ideas. Innovation should be encouraged and when it is, there is invariably a need for additional resources. The question is whether innovation strategies should be evaluated to determine their contribution to improved student outcomes. It seems self-evident that empirical evidence should demonstrate an agreed-upon return within a reasonable period of time.

An analysis of the assessments undertaken in this initiative demonstrated a lack of empirical data with inordinate use of satisfaction surveys. Commitments to evaluate an improved student achievement were conspicuously absent. But programs were operational and, once implemented, removing them was virtually impossible. This is a common situation facing government programs, and is a significant reason for increasing public sector debt.

Interestingly, the salaries of educators increased significantly during this same fourteen-year period. As already stated, inflation increased by 47 percent during these years, but salaries increased by 60 percent, or almost 1 percent beyond the annual inflation rate. Data revealed that educator's salaries increased in this province more than double that provided by another province with the next highest increase. Political leaders from the other provinces expressed their concern that this one province was needlessly driving up the cost of education across the country; this had a ripple effect that compelled governments elsewhere to increase their teacher salaries beyond what they deemed reasonable.

Unfortunately, the substantial increase in financial input did not result in a corresponding increase in student achievement. This region's performance on national and international assessments demonstrated a steady decline in reading and mathematics scores to the extent that ongoing visitations from other regions wanting to learn from previous levels of success virtually ended. Innovative international educators predictably reacted by voting with their feet: they knew that achievement was waning in spite of government funding increases, and they wanted to move to areas of the world where *student achievement remained the paramount concern.*

Perhaps an even more telling indicator of the decline occurred when the testing agency released the international comparative test scores. Rather than follow the province's traditional practice of holding a press conference to publicly celebrate success, they quietly released the disappointing results on a government website. Embarrassment and lack of transparency became the new norms.

Meanwhile, educators in this jurisdiction were happy because it meant more jobs, which provided them with more career options. Unions were happy because more educators in the system meant more union dues. Administrators were happy because more educators meant higher administrative allowances. Parents were happy because they believed their child was the recipient of special focus and attention. The public was happy because the government was spending more money on their community.

The culmination of all of this happiness was that politicians were happy because everyone else was happy and the prospect of reelection improved. The only fly in the ointment was that achievement was decreasing and few knew, and even fewer were upset enough to protest or take action. Common assessment linked with the Common Core provides our representatives in the political arena with critical information regarding whether programs should be retained. Relief for beleaguered taxpayers victimized by politicians' careless spending of other peoples' money can be achieved when program evaluation confirms that student achievement is not improving.

STANDARDIZED TESTS VILIFIED INAPPROPRIATELY

Standardized tests are now perceived as the villain because they are the messenger (Phelps 2003). They measure individual student achievement and provide the basis for assessing the individual teacher's contribution to student achievement. For the first time in the history of education, teacher performance is quantifiable, and, while not negating entirely the use of subjective measurement criteria, this largely numerical approach to describing performance is creating significant anxiety among teachers. In a workforce that considers job security a fundamental right, the idea that one could be demoted or even lose a job is almost unthinkable, even though it is the standard in much of the marketplace where teachers are served.

It is not surprising then that this possibility is attracting the overwhelming attention of teachers' unions. Using standardized tests to measure student learning has always concerned unions because they have understood that this carries with it the possibility of also measuring teacher quality. The National Education Association acknowledged this connection in a news release on its website on January 6, 2012:

NEA President Says Misuse of Standardized Tests Must Stop
High-stakes decisions based on bad tests hurt students and educators

WASHINGTON—January 6, 2012
No Child Left Behind (NCLB) has been a major factor in the proliferation of poor quality standardized tests. As we celebrate the 10th anniversary of the flawed legislation and as Congress prepares to reauthorize the law, NEA is urging careful consideration of the fact that these tests are being used to make high-stakes decisions about students' and teachers' futures and have corrupted the pursuit of improving real learning and effective teaching.

"When we use shoddy, fill-in-the bubble tests as the basis for an accountability system—tests that frequently aren't aligned with what's being taught in classrooms—so-called accountability systems lose all credibility," said NEA President Dennis Van Roekel. "It doesn't make sense to students, educators, parents, or credible testing experts, and now they're fighting back."

"Well-designed assessment systems do have a critical role in student success. We should use assessments to help students evaluate their own strengths and needs, and help teachers improve their practice and provide extra help to the students who need it."

As Congress continues to consider the reauthorization of the Elementary and Secondary Education Act (ESEA) and as state legislatures prepare to consider more education legislation this year, Van Roekel emphasized that NEA "remains hopeful that policy makers will wake up from the standardized test craze" and change policies to reflect what research has consistently shown: no single measure of either student learning or teacher performance can ever be the sole determinant of success or failure. Van Roekel stressed that we need robust assessment systems, designed to help all students –systems that make sense to students, parents, educators, and communities.

"High-stakes standardized tests that are used to punish students, teachers and schools, make testing companies more money, but they don't make students any smarter. Only good teaching, good parenting and good study habits will help ensure student success," said Van Roekel.

The union president made a significant statement when he said that "no single measure of either student learning or teacher performance can ever be the sole determinant of success or failure." *Until recently, teachers were the sole determinant of student learning, and their capacity to provide accurate assessments is significantly flawed. Principals were the sole determinants of teacher quality, and their conclusions have been questionable.* The primary point here is that the NEA is both acknowledging the need for an assessment of teachers' and linking it to student assessment.

The president also concluded his statement with a comment that standardized tests "don't make students any smarter." Teachers' unions added to this by saying that "just weighing a pig doesn't fatten it." These slogans are designed to confuse the public into thinking that standardized tests are inconsequential and a waste of time. Aside from developing this absurd metaphor, this comparison denigrates the important work that teachers do with children. Developing a child's mind to become a contributor in society should not be trivialized by comparing this task with fattening a pig.

To a pig farmer, weighing the pig can be important when attempting to determine which ingredients produce the greatest gain. Once the formula is developed, it can be used repeatedly. A child's brain is different. A formulated process for each child is unknown. Testing provides the intelligence that good teachers can use for determining their success in developing each child's capacity. Assessment provides teachers with knowledge regarding where teaching is required and where practice may need change.

The significant issue in this debate centers on the concept of "standardized testing." In simple terms, *standardized testing is any assessment given to two or more students.* With this understanding it is clearly evident that every teacher believes in standardized testing because they use this approach on a regular basis. Routinely teachers use tests on spelling and basic facts in mathematics. End-of-chapter and unit tests also qualify as standardized measurements in this simple definition of the concept, as do the myriad of worksheets utilized in classrooms on a daily basis.

Many tests are constructed wholly or in part by individual teachers who spend an hour or two on their local "standardized" test and seldom draw on best-practice principles. Professional test makers, by way of contrast, spend considerable time surveying classrooms for quality test items, which are then field-tested and the results carefully analyzed before the test is given in a process that takes up to a year to complete.

Therefore, standardized testing is not really the *villain* as far as teachers are concerned; rather, it is the fact that these tests are given to *more than one class of students at the same time. Comparability* of results between students in different classrooms is creating a high level of anxiety that is now evident across the education system. Comparability is the teachers' villain! It means that it is now possible to compare teachers' success and, therefore, to differentiate salaries and legitimately reward teachers on the basis of quantified effectiveness. As far as unions are concerned, these *messengers* of student learning must be vilified; otherwise the union will find it more difficult to protect members who fail to meet the standard.

The NEA's president also uses an overstatement to confuse the issue. Can these standardized tests be one of the measures? Is a comprehensive examination of student achievement important in evaluating students and their teachers, school, and school districts? The answer should be obvious, but the president implies that only one test is used to evaluate the teacher and therefore standardized tests are inappropriate. If the system was set up in the way the NEA intimates, it would be unfair for both students and teachers, but assessment is more complex than this. Statements like those of the president confuse and mislead the public.

John Bishop (2005) studied the effects of high school examinations in New York and concluded:

> Thirty percent of American teachers say they "feel pressure to give higher grades than students' work deserves" and "feel pressure to reduce the difficulty and amount of work you assign." Under a system of external exams, teachers and local school administrators lose the option of lowering standards to reduce failure rates and raise self-esteem. The only response open to them is to demand more of their students in order to maximize their chances of being successful on the external exams.

Bishop thus presents a powerful argument regarding the potential to reduce the tendency to inflate grades, which is so prevalent in our schools (and which will be covered in more detail later). He also summarized the results of the TIMSS as pointing to the benefits of standardized tests for students:

> Our review of the evidence suggests that the claims by advocates of standards based reform that curriculum-based external exit examinations significantly increase student achievement are probably correct. Students from countries with such systems outperform students from other countries at a comparable level of economic development by 1.3 grade equivalents in science and 1.0 grade equivalents in mathematics.

In Canada, all ten provinces participate in PISA every three years when the assessment is given. Over-sampling occurs within each province so that student results can be treated the same as national results for countries. Canada's educational system is unique because it is the only country in the developed world without a national office of education. Therefore its results are reported nationally as well as treating each province as a separate country.

Alberta has employed testing for all students in grades 3, 6, and 9 since 1995 and for grade 12 for more than a century. Its students performed at the first or second highest level among Canadian provinces on all three (reading, mathematics, and science) components in four PISA tests (2000, 2003, 2006, 2009). Its overall performance in 2003 was also at the highest level for any of the "nations" involved in PISA.

Manitoba began provincial testing at the same time as Alberta and ranked fourth overall among the ten provinces in PISA 2000. In 1999, an election promise to Manitoba's teachers to do away with compulsory testing precipitated a change in government. By the time their grade 3 students reached the age of fifteen and wrote the PISA 2009, this province's performance dropped to an overall Canadian ranking of ninth out of ten provinces. By not having provincial testing as a check and balance program for accountability, students in this province experienced a significant educational setback. In plain and simple language, the government failed its students and provided negative educational leadership for the province.

Meanwhile, Ontario ranked fifth overall in PISA 2000 when their provincial testing program began with assessments in reading and mathematics in grades 3, 6, and 9. Student achievement relative to the other provinces improved to an overall third place ranking in PISA 2009. In this instance, government leadership achieved greater levels of student success because it implemented provincial testing as a check and balance effort in accountability. Common assessment proved to be a successful technique for motivating educators to higher levels of performance.

One province, Prince Edward Island (PEI), was the last remaining Canadian province to incorporate large-scale testing in 2008. Student achievement as measured by PISA ranked ninth or tenth of ten provinces on the twelve tests from 2000 to 2009. The litmus test for common assessments' potential to leverage improved performance within that school system could be observed in succeeding years.

By 2013, a story of amazing success occurred within a jurisdiction habitually known to have the lowest levels of student achievement. Students' class marks were always high because standards employed by teachers were so low. Grade inflation hid the problems from citizens until common assessments across the country prodded the province's political arm into using common assessments across the province.

In the 2013 Canada-wide reading assessment, PEI moved upward to a sixth-place ranking of the ten provinces. Coincidentally, Manitoba, as predicted, dropped into last place while Ontario moved into first. In mathematics, PEI students achieved a fourth-place ranking while Manitoba placed a dismal last and Ontario placed second. In science, PEI placed sixth while Manitoba was last and Ontario was second. Predictions made years earlier were vindicated! PEI moved upward dramatically after incorporating common assessment while Manitoba flopped after dropping these assessments. Ontario's participation in common assessments also improved that province's rankings.

This Canadian data is noteworthy because it underscores the value for student achievement when common tests are utilized across the system. The trends evident reinforce the concept that *accountability is an investment and not an expense*. It is also noteworthy that the cost of each of Alberta's tests was less than $10 per student, which covered all elements of test preparation and marking. A relatively small investment in accountability packs a powerful punch in improvement. Large-scale assessment may be contentious with those seeking to avoid accountability, but its benefit in improving student achievement is worth the investment.

"NARROWING THE CURRICULUM" IS A MEANINGLESS SLOGAN

Teachers chafe at large-scale testing by claiming that tests "narrow the curriculum" and force them to "teach to the test." These slogans are intended to misguide the public and politicians, who may be too naïve to understand the ramifications. There is one aspect of the "narrowing the curriculum" argument that may have some validity but the criticism is misdirected. Phelps (2003) explains:

> Test critics commonly accuse high-stakes tests of "narrowing the curriculum," but it is actually the amount of time available that narrows it. In fact, all educators, including those opposed to standardized tests, narrow the curriculum. They have to. There is only so much instructional time available and choices must be made as to how that time is used. It is physically impossible to teach everything that can be possibly taught.

Education, over the course of many decades, added courses and content to school programs, but it avoided the difficult issue of negotiating contracts that would extend students' learning time and teachers' work year. *It is not surprising that many students struggle with their basic skills in such a crowded curriculum because politicians have avoided dealing with the difficult labor issues.* The point is that teachers are narrowing the curriculum not because of large-scale testing but because there is *insufficient time for dealing with the basic skills* in the program of studies coupled with many additional programs (for example, technology, fine arts, health, and safety).

State and national testing programs actually document the degree to which students are shortchanged in receiving basic education. When teachers argue that their testing programs force them to narrow their instruction to basic skills, poor results on system tests demonstrate that a poor job is being done to ensure mastery of basic skills. Imagine what the results would be if teachers were not concentrating on the basic skills that are deemed necessary for their students but not assessed on standardized tests.

The public should be thankful that the education system feels *pressure* to ensure that basic education is covered. Everyone should be focused on pursuing the goal of providing our children with sufficient time to cover basic education, as well as the plethora of content added to the curriculum since the time when we were an agrarian society. *We are unrealistic in thinking that today's students can be sufficiently prepared for tomorrow's world using "yesteryear's" time allocations.*

This issue of insufficient time to adequately accommodate new curricular components is confounded by *our need to have all students achieve graduation requirements.* One school administrator recalls a graduation address in the 1960s congratulating graduates on having achieved an education of the top 5 percent in the world. Obviously there were many underdeveloped places in the world where children did not even have access to education, but even in North America, many students dropped out of school prior to graduation.

Education Week provides evidence of U.S. graduation data indicating that completion rates peaked in 1969, with 77 percent of that high school class earning diplomas. This is the high point for American students achieving graduation. By 2007, the national graduation rate had fallen to 69 percent. Many children are being left behind in our transition from an agrarian to a technological society.

There are many other industrialized nations across the globe achieving higher graduation rates than the United States; however, *these nations do not have to construct physical barriers to keep people out*, such as occurs along the U.S. southern border. Those countries are not experiencing a significant influx of immigrants desperately seeking to achieve the American promise and improve their way of life. Without this confounding issue, America might also experience lower drop-out rates as occurs in Alberta, where fewer than 4 percent of students leave secondary school without achieving graduation.

The problem in our educational system is that we are "jamming" so much into the curriculum that many students are unable to keep pace. In 1870, 2 percent of American seventeen-year-olds achieved secondary school graduation. Many students dropped out after grade 8. The curriculum was so narrow in the agrarian era that people could function easily with knowing how to produce low-level work in the three "Rs"—Reading, wRiting, and aRithmetic.

Presumably, the 2 percent graduating at that time represented the nation's brightest and best students. Progressing to graduation rates of three-quarters and more of an entire population introduces a *significantly wider range of student abilities within our classrooms*. There are many students within this cohort requiring more than the hours currently provided in our schools to acquire the basic knowledge, skills, and attitudes required to live in our more complex world. Yet we expect that far less capable students will experience success on par with students who find school relatively easy.

This unrealistic expectation of our less capable students is the problem and a significant reason why educators feel they have to narrow the curriculum. In track events, for example, not everyone can run one hundred meters in less than ten seconds. Some will require twenty seconds or more to complete the journey, but they are not selected for Olympic tryouts. In school, not everyone can master today's updated and expanded curriculum in the thousand hours per year available to complete the educational journey. Of course, teachers feel pressure to narrow the curriculum, and that narrowing is focused on what is being measured: the curriculum that society, through its political institutions, has lawfully judged to being basic for an educated citizen.

EXPANDING ASSESSMENT

This "narrowing the curriculum" slogan is also used by educators to suggest that they are forsaking their responsibility to provide students with a well-rounded education, which includes subjects not assessed by large-scale tests. Some teachers say that they feel pressure to teach only the basics in reading, writing, and mathematics in order for students to demonstrate sufficient skill acquisition—that they do not have sufficient time to teach social studies, science, physical education, music, art, and so on. Yet all of these courses are part of a curriculum derived from a legal process involving public decisions and not from an arbitrarily imposed or whimsically chosen roster of esoteric subjects.

In other words, it is the law to teach all of these programs and no one has the prerogative of deciding to ignore their responsibility to teach them. Of course teachers feel pressure, or accountability, for ensuring that their students achieve basic skills that are necessary to succeed in our society. Choosing to avoid their responsibility for teaching other subject matter is a dereliction of duty that should be a matter of discipline. Of course, this would require administrators to monitor the degree to which teachers disregard their legal responsibilities.

This language may sound harsh to someone unfamiliar with the nuances of this debate. It is somewhat understandable that teachers might choose to concentrate on what is tested and measured. *The answer to this dilemma is not to do away with large-scale assessment but to expand it.* Every aspect of the curriculum should be assessed to ensure that students are taught the full program of studies, and that it is taught well.

With so much evidence demonstrating the value of large-scale assessment in improving student achievement, teachers' unions should demand its greater use and thereby demonstrate their service orientation for students. Instead of resisting administrators, they should be working with them to correct the problems that proper assessment reveals. When issues are identified in a normal cycle of standardized testing, they should exercise leadership that helps weak performers rather than excusing or shielding them.

If unions are genuinely interested in student success, they should be clamoring to have large-scale assessment expanded to subjects not currently undergoing systematic assessment. There is too much evidence indicating that teachers concentrate more on subjects where large-scale assessment occurs to the detriment of other subjects where it is not—for example, art, physical education, and music. These programs are important and should be valued with the same expectations accorded to reading, writing, mathematics, social studies, and science.

One parent recorded observations he made about the performance of physical education programs in his child's school. Few parents are permitted to observe teachers across their classes inside the school building. Parking his car outside of school playgrounds, and observing for quality of programs not included in the system's assessment program, he noted huge variations. This experience helped him understand the value in using assessment as a tool for improving all aspects of schooling.

Given what we know today about accountability and assessment, teachers should be demanding that subjects not being currently tested, because they are difficult to assess with paper and pencil, be assessed in some other *standardized* way. It may be more costly, but group work, public speaking, and listening are skills that can and should be assessed, and the results could be used to improve instruction.

In other words, it is unconscionable that the school system, which knows what will help students, refuses to advocate for these changes because of self-interest. This is particularly distressing because it means that the system cannot help teachers who could be helped if there were openness and transparency. Elevating the importance of all subjects is a laudable objective.

Every student is entitled to learn the full curriculum, and learn it well. Every parent deserves to have their child provided with the skills, knowledge, and attitudes of the entire educational program. Taxpayers and their governments are entitled to have their investments provide all students with an education deemed necessary for living successfully. We want everyone to contribute to our society in a meaningful way. *It is an affront when educators choose to subvert their legal obligations by reducing their teaching in non-tested programs because they want to look good in the areas measured by large-scale assessments.*

The foregoing is not promoting "paper and pencil" tests as the only way for assessing student learning. Assessments of student learning can occur when students demonstrate talent for teamwork, creativity, physical, and musical ability, second language, speaking, and so on. While it is necessary to assess individual students in the basic curriculum, random samples can be applied in other areas. This procedure may be especially important during the introductory phase while we learn how to best assess these additional areas.

Skeptics might oppose efforts to increase assessment to all aspects of the curriculum because accountability could then be applied to all teachers in the school in addition to those teaching subjects currently being tested. Schools would experience productive pressure to ensure that all students receive a quality education in all areas, including in some subjects that teachers are teaching but in which they are not particularly talented. Many students are shortchanged by their placement with teachers who lack specific qualification, interest, or talent but are forced by circumstances to nevertheless teach the class.

One principal acknowledged this concern but indicated how he resolved it so that all students would have the opportunity to participate in a high-quality program. Rather than require each teacher to be proficient in all aspects of the curriculum, he banded together with other schools so that teachers became subject specialists. Teachers might teach the same subject across all grades in one or more schools. Their preparations were greatly reduced to just one subject, and they only had to learn curricular components in one subject area. Such platooning is common in middle and high schools, and there is no reason why younger students should not receive the benefits of instruction from an expert.

The superintendent responsible for this group of schools soon shared in the excitement because student achievement on the standardized testing program demonstrated significant improvement. Imagination in creative problem solving by school principals enhanced the program for all students so that none were disadvantaged by being placed with an unqualified or disinterested teacher.

"TEACHING TO THE TEST" IS ILL-CONCEIVED RHETORIC

The public's confusion regarding large-scale testing is also heightened by the educators' slogan about "teaching to the test." This saying is as misguided as "narrowing the curriculum." It is absurd to test what is not taught. It is only fair to students that they be taught what is going to be tested. Vociferous and legitimate objections would be voiced if students were tested on content not contained within the curriculum.

In the period of time before states implemented large-scale testing programs, educators used generic tests from testing companies, which were not curriculum specific. These generic tests were developed to accommodate the largest populated regions, such as California in the United States and Ontario in Canada. Yes, most of the test items did fit the curricula of other regions, but there always were some questions that were not a perfect match.

While teachers used these generic tests for their own purposes, they objected to any attempt to hold them accountable for the results because some questions did not relate to their state's curriculum. This proved to be a convenient dodge for any accountability and led to today's testing programs, where states develop their own tests to match their curriculum.

So if teachers object to "teaching to the test," what are they teaching? If the test is derived from the lawful curriculum, why is this being ridiculed? The reason why so many states went through the arduous process of building curriculum frameworks in the 1990s was to ensure that all aspects of their curriculum were taught. Instructional omissions occurred because teachers were choosing to teach their preferred curriculum sometimes to the exclusion of that mandated by the state. Instead of "teaching *to* the test," should teachers "teach *away* from the test"?

Phelps (2003) provides a cogent description of the illogical situation taken by anti-testing advocates:

> "Teaching to the test" is the perfect "damned if you do, damned if you don't" argument. Do not teach the material that will be covered in a test, and you will be excoriated. Teach what will be covered in a test, and you will be excoriated. The only way out, of course, is the solution preferred by testing opponents—stop all testing (and let them run the schools the way they like).

There is significant insight in the final phrase: "let them run the schools the way they like." A subsequent chapter in this book deals with the incursion and intrusion of social promotion into educational practice. When students are shuffled through our schools without demonstrating sufficient learning and understanding of the curriculum, teachers are forced to adapt the curriculum to meet their students' academic needs.

Curriculum adaptation is good practice for some, but too many students are experiencing social promotion because the school system lost its accountability for ensuring that students are ready for the next grade. Too many teaching practices are employed without a database supporting their use. Too many effective organizational practices are disregarded and not implemented.

Tests expose this lack of success. Tests reveal that there are differences in teacher quality. Tests demonstrate that some schools are more effective than others. Tests provide indication that some students are disadvantaged by elements within their educational system. Tests make teachers, principals, system administrators, and politicians accountable for their leadership. They put pressure on these levels of leadership to employ meaningful improvement strategies. *They are our messengers of excellence and mediocrity*, which is the reason why some want them "killed." They are "messengers" that expose shortcomings and make the system feel uncomfortable. Hence the name of Phelps's book: *Kill the Messenger*.

"Teaching *to* the test" is not the real issue. What is objectionable is when teachers "teach the test." Some testing programs use the same tests for several administrations, and it is possible that some teachers access the questions unethically and use these actual questions for review in subsequent years before the questions are released for public use. This practice is cheating because it is *teaching the test*, literally.

What is upside-down in these slogans, used by unions and educators, misrepresents aspects of assessment in an attempt to avoid accountability for providing students with an excellent education. They should be advocating that all aspects of the curriculum be assessed rather than not having any assessment. They should be promoting fairness to students by insisting that gains in student achievement be consistently and persistently monitored so that no one falls through the cracks. They should be advocating that schools provide more hours for instruction so that *pace of learning* can be accommodated.

Politicians' sympathy for the incoherent arguments of anti-testing proponents exposes their priorities. Rather than implementing testing programs that will ensure greater fairness for students across the educational system, they placate educators seeking to absent themselves from accountability for student achievement. By pledging their allegiance to the service providers, they demonstrate an attitude opposed to student's best interests.

Increasing student access to instructional time may make for messy negotiations, but today's living is more complex than yesterdays. Expecting every student to learn at the "superstar" rate is unrealistic. There are 8,760 hours in a year, and using only 1,000 hours (or 12 percent of the year) for education is insufficient and impractical for our nation's future well-being. Maintaining a teacher work year that supported our agrarian economy is no longer sufficient. Slavish adherence to old-fashioned organizational aspects of schooling is unconscionable.

In the political arena it is all about gaining and retaining power. Politicians look to survive the next political test, which is an election sometime within the next four years. Educators comprise a relatively large voting bloc of between 1 and 2 percent of the population and, since children are ineligible, a larger percentage of voters. Educators' votes can be the key to an election victory and holding political office.

There is a need for politicians to counter the snappy slogans craftily prepared to confuse the public. If they are unwilling to be the messengers of fact, then they need to empower their bureaucrats to participate in the public debate. Rather than pander for teacher votes, politicians need to pander for public support by ensuring its education regarding how the nation's future is jeopardized.

Common Core provides the means for comparing state results in student achievement so that some accountability or pressure is exerted to raise standards. Common assessment provides the measurement for ensuring that standards are achieved. Therefore, they are a relatively low-cost investment for demonstrating to the public that their investment in education is maximized. Comparability of results is not bad! Rather than attempting to "kill the messenger," politicians should be focused on providing students with greater fairness whether it be through more effective service from the education system or more reliable assessments from their teachers.

The key points made in this chapter are as follows:

- Teachers are supporting Common Core but resisting common assessment.
- No child in any school will be more accountable than the adults in the system.
- Anecdotal evidence from many teachers indicates how infrequently they ever see their principal in their classroom.
- Students have their work inspected and assessed much more frequently than occurs with teachers.
- Teacher evaluations are meaningless because they do not differentiate talent or monitor degrees of success.
- It is also necessary to hold school administrators to a higher level of accountability than their teachers.
- A critical point is that common assessment of student achievement potentially alters the dynamics of how educators—teachers and administrators—are evaluated.
- Common assessment linked with Common Core alters the prevailing dynamics in education where popularity is more important than performance.
- When it is determined that an initiative truly has value in terms of improving outcomes, it is logical to expect that a school would retain the program and find funding by withdrawing resources from other programs where "bang for the buck" is less. Seldom does this exchange occur.
- Until recently, teachers were the sole determinants of student learning, and their capacity to provide accurate assessments is significantly flawed. Principals were the sole determinants of teacher quality, and their conclusions are questionable.
- Standardized testing is not really the *villain* as far as teachers are concerned; rather, it is the fact that these tests are given to more than one class of students at the same time.
- Accountability through common assessment is an investment and not an expense.
- "Narrowing the Curriculum" and "Teaching to the Test" are meaningless slogans attempting to confuse the public.

NINE

Paying Teachers for What Matters

Discussing teacher pay within the context of Common Core may appear senseless to many; however, the relevance between these two concepts is high. Support among educators for common standards across participating states remains fairly constant; however, opposition to outcomes attached to this initiative is building. Eventually, Common Core provides an opportunity to transform how educators are paid.

Chapter 4 describes games played by presidential candidates seeking the White House in 2016 and how nonsensical are the positions they espouse while trying to avoid being labeled Common Core supporters. Frequently their stated positions are based on arguments demonstrated to be erroneous while the wiggle room they invent borders on the laughable. These politicians endeavor to pander to special interest groups, not the least of whom are teachers.

Most of the declared presidential candidates for 2016 are Republican, and so the Democrats' early standard bearer, specifically Hillary Clinton, refrains from saying too much. Until another legitimate Democratic opponent emerges, *she can afford to waltz through the primaries without declaring a position on Common Core and without offending voters who might be or might become her supporters.* In the early stages in this run for the White House, candidates articulate many conflicting views concerning Common Core, which makes this issue sufficiently contentious and a legitimate election issue.

While the media's attention on Common Core is focused primarily on reporting how it is splitting the Republican candidates, Democrats are escaping from any exposure on an equally contentious circumstance. Accountability, a longstanding touchstone for Republicans, is receiving scant attention from the media because Hillary Clinton has little opposition in the early stage and her Republican opponents are preoccupied with other philosophical matters related to constitutionality. Whether the debate on Common Core ever focuses on its potential to achieve high levels of accountability in the education system remains to be seen.

COMMON CORE REQUIRES COMMON ASSESSMENT

Common Core could be neutralized as an election issue if the Republican candidate emerging from the primaries as a contender for the presidency is one *who traded support for this initiative away for votes.* Should this be the case, the *Democratic candidate will dodge a significant bullet in dealing with the important accountability issue of teachers' pay.* In its early years, teachers supported Common Core, but their opposition to common assessment is fierce because of its connection with how teachers are to be evaluated and then paid.

This book clearly endorses Common Core because it offers critical accountability in education across the United States. *Politicians wrangle over falsities, to the detriment of a precious education principle: providing an accountability platform that ensures fairness to America's students.* American politics must transcend petty bickering over what is *inconsequential* and embrace what is in the best interests of students. *Governors from both sides of the political spectrum chose a vision wisely* when they triggered this educational reform for the benefit of students.

A second critical message in this book pertains to the vision of attaching common assessment to Common Core, which is not only a natural fit but also a must. It is common sense that all students across participating states are able to demonstrate the same high standards, and there should be no tolerance for second-rate learning. When this principle is accepted, a dramatic step toward fairness for all students is possible; however, it can be readily overturned by not embracing common assessment.

In chapter 2 we documented the fraudulent behavior of states during their quest to achieve NCLB's annual improvement targets. *Without common assessments, states had flexibility to choose their tests and, subsequently, reduce difficulty levels resulting in a naïve public believing that student achievement was improving.* This unfortunate lesson reminds us that negating common standards is relatively easy to accomplish; yet undoing its purpose is easy to prevent with the adoption of common assessment. *In fact, without common assessment there will be no Common Core.*

Fairness to students requires Common Core in order that all learners achieve high standards regardless of race, background, or location. This principle of fairness must be attached to an accountability based on common assessments in order that everyone—taxpayers, students, parents, politicians, and educators—have a common understanding regarding the degree of learning taking place. An expectation for high standards must be accompanied by a measurement program that provides quantitative evidence that achievement across the participating states is at high levels.

TEACHER PAY

Accountability is a significant issue in education as it is throughout the public sector. When it comes to determining pay, people, including educators, *should be paid for what really matters: student learning and success.* Teachers are notoriously defensive whenever their pay is discussed, and educators reading this chapter's title likely expect comments about issues such as benefits, length of work year, comparisons with other types of work, working conditions, and so on. These issues may provoke interesting discussions but are not the subject in this chapter; rather, the intent is to examine the basis upon which teachers are remunerated and whether current assumptions are valid.

Teacher salaries are complicated by the philosophical assumptions embedded within union agreements. One of the most pernicious is that all participants in the grid should receive the same compensation, which means that teachers working in a region with the same level of education and years of experience receive the same compensation. While there are early signs that the situation is changing in parts of the United States, this approach prevents employers from recognizing, rewarding, or incentivizing talent. *Compensation should recognize contribution toward student success*, and the educational system is prevented from celebrating teacher worth in enhancing this success.

Jensen and Reichl (2011) studied the value of current processes designed to recognize teacher success, and conclude that appraisal and feedback is *ineffective*:

Teachers' appraisal doesn't improve teaching: over 60% of teachers report that appraisal of their work has little impact on the way they teach in the classroom. . . . Teacher appraisal is just an administrative exercise with no feedback to improve student performance: over 60% of teachers report that appraisal of their work is largely done simply to fulfill administrative requirements. . . . Effective teaching is not recognized: over 90% of teachers report that the most effective teachers in their school do not receive the greatest recognition, and that if they improved the quality of their teaching they would not receive any recognition.

These authors remind us that our current system of appraising teachers is ineffective and that superior teachers are not rewarded, *and improving teachers would not be appropriately recognized.* Union agreements that treat everyone the same run counter to how people should be recognized and rewarded. Common Core combined with common assessment provides a means for addressing this longstanding ineffective practice.

In the case of most teachers, there is a base pay earned by qualifying to teach, and then there are supplements that teachers receive as they acquire additional university degrees and experience. *In fact, we can generalize that teachers receive a bonus for acquiring additional certification and getting older on the job.* These two criteria are the basis for pay differentiation and reward. Until recently, job performance was irrelevant and these two criteria supposedly differentiated who were the better teachers.

The current debate on teacher pay is gaining prominence because of the use of standardized testing across the United States. Previous attempts to implement merit pay schemes largely failed because assessments of teacher performance were subjective and based on the school principal's evaluation of a teacher. Too many differences in opinion regarding a teacher's competence were evident, and there was too little agreement on which competencies mattered. *Subjectivity encourages bias, which leads to unfairness, regardless of whether the assessment is about teacher performance or student learning.*

Rather than recognize classroom performance and student success, in particular, merit pay programs focused on a teacher's contribution *outside of their classroom.* For example, teachers might earn favor with their principals if they assumed additional responsibilities such as coaching students or leading professional development activities for teacher colleagues. These duties are helpful in the school, but *success in teaching students should always be the final arbiter in determining worth, and therefore salary.* We hire teachers to teach the school curriculum to students.

When school districts first introduced merit-based pay scales, which focused on individual activity rather than group success, benefits were limited. A sense of teamwork was lost and a competitive teacher environment developed. There were winners and losers because the amount of money available was limited, and teachers recognized that if they helped a colleague, it might be to their own detriment. Team orientation, which is so necessary in a school environment where staffs are encouraged to learn from each other, was replaced by attitudes of distrust and rivalry.

This new focus on the individual made it almost impossible for those making decisions about awarding pay to measure impact because several teachers were involved with the same student, while many others were not involved in ways that permitted assessment. *In its earliest renditions, merit pay failed to gain traction because it could not isolate individual contributions and undervalued group performance.*

The necessary preconditions for merit pay were not yet in the system. Without standardized forms of measurement, evaluations had to focus on *raw* scores rather than *gains*. The former is confounded by the student's socioeconomic status, which is beyond the school's control. The latter is what matters. The critical question—and the one that should impact pay—is whether the *student has experienced a gain, and this is within the power of a school to produce.*

From a political perspective, implementing merit pay was important but for the wrong reason. At a time when there were calls for increased accountability in education, school systems pointed to merit pay schemes as a step in that direction. Politicians secured community support by demonstrating a commitment to greater accountability, which could also lever additional funding from governments to satisfy special interest groups. There was justification to spend more, ostensibly because there was greater accountability in schools.

Tim Pawlenty, once governor of Minnesota and later candidate for president of the United States, understood the connection between common assessment and teacher accountability. In a visit to my jurisdiction he asked the critical question: Is annual testing of student learning required for teacher accountability? Without this provision of annual assessment, determining each teacher's contribution becomes impossible. Teachers in grades without assessment do not feel the same level of accountability because blame or credit for student success can be assigned to the teacher of the grade tested.

PERFORMANCE EVALUATIONS

The advent of standardized testing changed the landscape because it raised the prospect of rewarding teachers as well as their educational leaders. However, as was noted above, the teachers' unions strongly opposed standardized testing, seeing the introduction of such tests as a threat to the comfort and security that teachers enjoyed.

The main focus of a teachers' union is the welfare of its members, and the current approaches to evaluating teacher performance are so nebulous that any conclusion is difficult to substantiate. This potential for subjectivity in evaluating teacher performance is a significant aspect in maintaining secure employment for educators. The many legal loopholes, when subjectivity is involved, make it difficult to prove a definitive case of incompetence.

Any subjective statement can be challenged because it is usually a perception based on observation. One superintendent indicated that their principal's qualifications on a teacher's "less than satisfactory" evaluation were challenged on the witness stand by lawyers, who focused on technical errors in the principal's report. Their argument was that if an administrator, with several university degrees, was unable to write a properly constructed sentence, he or she must be unable to accurately assess teacher performance.

Furthermore, was the evaluator emphasizing the most significant elements of effective instruction? Teacher strength in some elements might compensate for weaknesses in others. Who could be absolutely certain as to which *inputs* provided the line of demarcation necessary for verifying quality performance? There are myriad teaching elements to consider in each skill that is used to create an effective classroom. There is considerable difficulty in basing performance evaluations on teaching processes, when the interplay of these processes is so important and complex.

For this reason, classroom control and discipline became the most critical element of instruction, because they were the deficiencies most easily observed. How could learning take place in an unruly environment? Teachers soon caught on to this focus and devised all sorts of strategies to ensure that students were well behaved when supervisors entered the sanctity of their classrooms. Students were taught how to demonstrate exemplary behavior in front of visitors, including the principal who likely was conducting an evaluation.

In another instance, the principal met all of the procedures in the evaluation process culminating with a meeting to inform the teacher that his performance was deemed to be "less than satisfactory." One procedural glitch occurred at the final moment because the report was supposed to be filed in an administrative office by midnight on April 30. It was not. Rather, it arrived eight hours later, and this procedural misstep negated further action for another year.

These examples demonstrate how easily it is to avoid dismissing a poor teacher and why subjectively based assessments too frequently take the assessor and the assessed down a blind alley. Reeder (2005) undertook an extensive review of legal bills incurred by school districts when attempting to dismiss tenured teachers. His report expresses the experience of many school districts, and he concludes with the following:

> Bills indicate schools districts have spent an average of $219,504.21 in legal fees for dismissal cases and related litigation from the beginning of 2001 until the end of 2005. As staggering as that number is, it actually understates the ultimate cost of these lawsuits because 44 percent of these cases are still on appeal and the lawyer bills continue to grow. Cost is a major reason cited by school officials for not trying to dismiss underperforming teachers, said T.J. Wilson, a Monticello attorney specializing in education labor law. "There is always the possibility that the school district may have to cut some program that benefits children, just to pay for the cost of firing a teacher. This is the biggest reason school districts do not try to fire bad teachers." In fact, in the last 18 years, 93 percent of Illinois school districts have never attempted to fire anyone with tenure, according to data tabulated from records at the Illinois State Board of Education.

Not documented in Reeder's report is the amount of administrator time involved in various hearings related to a dismissal. Frequently, these hearings occur during the summer months, requiring principals and superintendents to cancel vacation plans in order to be available for several days of grilling to justify their recommendation for termination. The significant costs in money and time leave many unwilling to tackle classroom incompetence. As a result, unions can easily protect their members and prove to them that they were more than adequate in looking after everyone's well-being. *Their success may not have been in students' best interests, but that is not their primary interest.*

TEACHER EVALUATIONS BASED ON EMPIRICAL EVIDENCE

Standardized testing introduces objectivity to the process, which, in turn, upsets the applecart to such a degree that opposition from teachers is gaining momentum. By focusing on outcomes related to student achievement rather than on inputs of teaching style, evaluation is focused on what matters: *impact rather than activity.* There is no need to determine the relative merit of various aspects of teaching style. What matters most is the value being added in student learning by the teacher's effort and talent. Is it positive or negative relative to expectations? Is a student's achievement improving and is the improvement sufficient?

The importance of introducing empirical evidence should not be underestimated. Unions have consistently attempted to deflect criticism of those teachers who received "less than satisfactory" evaluations. However, *today school administrators are replacing uncertainty about their conclusions with empirical evidence of teacher effectiveness beyond classroom management data.* The union has the burden of proof in refuting a conclusion that is viewed as measuring the bottom line of teaching. Through this change, student outcomes rather than teacher inputs are the focus for analysis and evaluation.

A Canadian study in 2005 undertaken by the *Society for the Advancement of Excellence in Education* found high levels of parental support for using standardized test results in teacher evaluations. Seventy-three percent of parents supported this approach, whereas only 67 percent trusted the traditional approach of relying on a principal's evaluation. Not surprisingly, only 28 percent of Canadian teachers agreed that evaluations should utilize standardized test results.

A recent Gallup Poll in the United States assessed American attitudes to the same issue, but with an interesting difference. In their 2012 *Phi Delta Kappan* publication, the pollsters asked, "In your opinion, what percentage of a teacher's evaluation should be based on how well his or her students perform on standardized tests—less than one-third, between one-third and two-thirds, or more than two-thirds?" *Eighty-three percent of American adults supported having more than one-third of the teacher's evaluation based on test results.*

Acting on this high level of support, President Obama's Race to the Top initiative provided incentives to states to withdraw legislation that *forbade the use of standardized test results in teacher evaluations and replace it with legislation that mandated their use.* It is incredible that politicians in some states actually opposed evaluating teachers on the basis of student achievement. Given the degree of support for linking teacher evaluations to measures of student achievement, it is only a matter of time before this becomes the norm rather than the exception.

While this debate intensifies, it is important that decision-makers consider carefully what aspects of standardized test results should be used. Unions are attempting to discredit their use on the basis that test results are impacted by the socioeconomic status of a region. And this is true. Disadvantaged children do not achieve as well as their advantaged peers. If evaluations were based on *raw score* results, teachers would abandon working in schools that serve disadvantaged populations.

The intent, instead, should be to focus on the *gain* in student scores. The question should be, "To what extent has the student demonstrated improved achievement since the beginning of the school year?" This focus on gain scores neutralizes the effect of socioeconomic conditions, so that teachers do not have to worry about which community their school serves.

Considerable attention is given to this nuanced use of standardized testing in teacher evaluation and salary scales because teachers' unions have been so energetic in attempting to confuse the public. Moving toward a focus on student learning and away from teacher activity, which may or may not contribute to student learning, is a contentious issue, and the battle is heating up. Dobbins and Bentsen (2014) provide a concise summary of the controversy:

> Bill Gates said that education reform is more difficult than eradicating polio, malaria or tuberculosis. He supports all of these causes, but the Common Core State Standards (CCSS) Initiative that he helped spearhead is coming under increasing criticism. . . . The backlash against Common Core has grown steadily since states first implemented the initiative, and now teachers' unions are withdrawing their support because of its increased teacher accountability requirements. . . . Teachers' unions across the United States are using this period of reform to try to modify or remove value-added measures—algorithms that link teacher evaluations to student performance—under No Child Left Behind. States agreed to these value-added accountability evaluations for stu-

dents and teachers in exchange for federal funding th[r]ough the Race to the Top program. Student outcomes on CCSS exams are tied to teacher evaluations. Teachers whose students do not achieve "success" on the CCSS annual exam are labeled "ineffective."

A prominent economist and education reformer, Eric Hanushek (2014), adds,

> Educational improvement requires strong accountability systems, rewarding teachers who are effective, eliminating teachers who are harming students, and providing added choice to parents about where their children go to school. Research has shown that these policies, while not silver bullets, each push toward higher student achievement.

The teachers' unions advocate revoking the most critical component of improving student achievement: teacher accountability ratings. At their national convention, the American Federation of Teachers (AFT), the second largest teachers' union in the United States, discussed how they would oppose and/or reform Common Core, having called for a moratorium on the accountability standards. The AFT would like to rewrite the Common Core standards as well as *remove testing measurements that hold teachers accountable for student performance.*

National Education Association president Eskelsen Garcia calls value-added measures a "mark of the devil" (Dobbins and Bentsen 2014). A reasonable person recognizes that using student gain scores as a measure of teacher performance is far more credible than dismissing this approach with such a farcical metaphor. Garcia's "over the top" description is absurd!

UNWINDING THE MYTH ABOUT EXTRINSIC MOTIVATION

Because the desire to link teachers' salaries to student achievement represents a serious threat to the status quo, unions have raised another objection in an effort to discredit its use and the use of other private sector motivational strategies in the safe confines of the public sector. Teachers' unions want the public to believe that extrinsic motivation is incongruent in the school because it is seen as being manipulative and counterproductive. They assert that intrinsic motivation is sufficient. Teachers' satisfaction needs are supposedly achieved through the joy of working with our nation's youth.

In other words, paying teachers on the basis of their performance evaluation, which includes a component related to student achievement, is not necessary. Indeed, some may say that it is not necessary to reward their efforts with financial incentives; however, they are rewarded for getting older on the job and achieving additional certification.

Yet teachers utilize extrinsic motivation with their students constantly in their classrooms by giving out stickers, awards, prizes, and public praise. If anything, it may be that teachers, more than any other group of professionals, understand the value of extrinsic motivation, which may make them more sensitive when it is utilized in their work environment.

Cameron and Pierce (2002), who were well aware of the controversy within education, provided a historical perspective:

> Although the claim that rewards have general negative effects is popular, it is also wrong because it is based on an idealistic and faulty view of human nature. . . . Although the findings from the initial studies were weak and inconclusive, they are frequently cited as evidence that rewards have generalized negative effects on human behavior. This view has been touted for the past three decades in newspaper articles, major psychology textbooks, education and business journals, and many other outlets. . . . The notion that rewards sap people's intrinsic motivation can be understood as an off-shoot of other sentiments and concerns that were popular in the 1960's and 1970's.

Is it possible that the social environment leading to the "hippie generation" influenced people's perspective concerning extrinsic rewards? The private sector shuns this view with its work force, but the public sector seems inadequate in becoming enlightened.

Cameron and Pierce went on to clarify the following points:

- Rewards tied to success, gradual challenge, and mastery can enhance measures of intrinsic motivation.
- What is clear is that rewards and other reinforcements do not have inherent negative effects on human motivation.
- Behavior is, in fact, extensively regulated by its effects. Actions that bring rewards are generally repeated, whereas those that bring unrewarding or punishing outcomes tend to be discarded.
- Achievement-based rewards help people to develop personal control over outcomes, adopt challenging personal standards, and learn to make a positive self-evaluation of their accomplishments.

- Extrinsic rewards given for merely doing an interesting activity repeatedly are most likely to reduce intrinsic interest. Rewards given for mastery (i.e., achieving relatively challenging behavioral standards) are the type of reward contingency that is said to develop perceptions of self-efficacy and task interest.
- Rewards given for meeting or exceeding a challenging criterion verify people's competence. Rewards tied to achieving performance objectives also cause people to care more about doing well at an activity and increase intrinsic interest more than positive performance feedback without reward.

CURRENT PAY BONUSES ARE WRONGHEADED

Having outlined the need to use empirical data in evaluating a teacher and then the need to take results into consideration when determining an appropriate salary for the teacher, it still remains necessary to debunk another pernicious idea that plagues the system: paying teachers for getting older and acquiring more education also perpetuates ineffectiveness and is an illustration of the upside-down reality that exists in North American education. *These two aspects have been in use for decades and have cost taxpayers large sums of money, but without justification.* Indeed, the focus contributed to less than excellent service for our children because teachers are rewarded for things that do not yield results.

Educators are like other humans and respond positively to extrinsic motivation such as pay. Actually, extrinsic motivation in the form of money is already evident in the current payment program for teachers where they are incentivized to pursue additional degrees. Research studies found that more teachers pursued additional degrees in regions where these garnered greater increases in salary. Additional remuneration is a sufficient incentive or bonus for many teachers to acquire a master's degree.

Since teachers receive a bonus beyond their base pay if they successfully acquire additional certification, the critical question is whether it makes a difference in their performance. Does the additional certification improve their ability to teach so that students learn better?

Hughes-Jones et al. (2006) examined the issue of certification across three U.S. states and concluded that "teachers' graduate degrees had no significant effect on student achievement." Buddin and Zamarro (2009) reviewed several criteria used for determining teacher pay and concluded:

> Teacher effectiveness is typically measured by traditional teacher qualification standards, such as experience, education, and scores on licensure examinations. RAND researchers found no evidence that these standards have a substantial effect on student achievement in Los Angeles public elementary, middle, and high schools. Alternative measures of teacher qualifications and different kinds of reward systems might be more effective at improving teacher quality. Traditional teacher qualifications have little influence on classroom achievement. . . . When the researchers analyzed student achievement data along with teacher qualifications, they found that a five-year increase in teaching experience affected student achievement very little—less than 1 percentage point. Similarly, the level of education held by a teacher proved to have no effect on student achievement in the classroom.

Harris and Sass (2008) conducted their analysis of experience and certification indicating that increased certification may even have a *negative effect* on student achievement.

> Like other recent work, we find generally positive, but mixed, evidence on the effects of experience and little or no evidence of the efficacy of advanced degrees for teachers. We find that the first few years of experience substantially increase the productivity of elementary and middle school teachers but have little impact on the effectiveness of teachers at the high school level. Only in the case of middle school math do we find that obtaining an advanced degree enhances the ability of a teacher to promote student achievement. For all other grade/subject combinations the correlation between advanced degrees and student achievement is negative or insignificant.

Greene (2005) examined the certification issue, labeling it a *myth,* and summarized his review regarding the importance of experience on teaching effectiveness:

> *Abell Foundation* found that teachers holding master's degrees did not produce higher student performance (except for high school teachers with master's degrees in the subjects they taught, as opposed to degrees in education). The evidence seems to indicate that teachers get a little more effective in their first few years as they get up to speed in the classroom, but that after this initial period teachers do not tend to get more effective with more years of experience.

Goe and Stickler (2008) similarly assessed the value of teachers pursuing additional certification and concluded:

> The effects associated with a teacher's possession of an advanced degree are strikingly counterintuitive, especially given the salary incentives offered to encourage teachers to pursue graduate degrees. Not only do recent empirical studies not find a substantial benefit for students of teachers with advanced degrees, but the majority of such studies also indicate that teachers with master's degrees and beyond may negatively influence their student's achievement.

Roza and Miller (2009) differentiated the value of pursuing additional certification between subject areas and reported:

> On average, master's degrees in education bear no relation to student achievement. Master's degrees in math and science have been linked to improved student achievement in those subjects, but 90 percent of teachers' master's degrees are in education programs—a notoriously unfocused and process-dominated course of study. Because of the financial rewards associated with getting this degree, the education master's experienced the highest growth rate of all master's degrees between 1997 and 2007.
>
> Divestment should be part of an effort to distribute compensation differently, in ways that offer greater benefit to students. Teachers currently finance their master's degree studies in anticipation of guaranteed financial returns, but if teachers anticipated higher pay based instead on enhanced ability to boost student achievement, their interests would be better aligned with those of their students.
>
> In the fiscal climate ahead, school systems serious about improving results for students will have no choice but to reconsider their long-automated ways of spending money, uncover how much money is at stake, and compare current ways of spending to alternative ones with greater potential to benefit to students.

We could go on at great length about these two issues and the rewards they bring. What is noteworthy is the absence of research that justifies the use of increased experience beyond the first couple of years and the acquisition of additional degrees as a reward for excellent service. Michael Bamesberger reported in the *Daily Nebraskan* (2011) the conclusions of the U.S. secretary of education as well as those of an American philanthropist:

> In November [2010], U.S. Education Secretary Arne Duncan singled out the $8 billion spent on master's degree bonuses annually as waste-

ful, claiming there is "little evidence teachers with master's degrees improve students' achievement more than other teachers," according to a speech he gave to the American Enterprise Institute. Microsoft founder Bill Gates also came out in opposition to the bonuses, citing a University of Washington study in which master's degrees in education were found to bear no relation to student achievement.

While the issue of pay receives considerable attention in the United States, a few Canadian studies support American findings. In 1997–1999, Canada tested students in reading, mathematics, and science, and collected survey results from students and teachers. Using the teacher data and measuring the performance of students scoring at level three—the passing score—or better, Alberta's students scored the highest and had the greatest percentage of teachers with *less* than five years of post-secondary education. Coincidentally, Alberta's teachers had the lowest pay differential between a bachelor's and a second degree. By implication, therefore, teachers in Alberta were less motivated by degrees and experience than were teachers in other jurisdictions.

A few years later, in 2007, the Council of Ministers' Education Canada undertook another review of student achievement in reading relative to teacher education levels. In this instance, students with teachers possessing a B.Ed. degree and some additional non-formal training scored significantly higher than did students in classes where the teacher possessed a graduate degree. One explanation for this counterintuitive result is that teachers with advanced degrees may become more interested in advancing their careers through administration rather than advancing skills for the classroom. Coursework then may be a distraction to their efforts in acquiring classroom expertise.

This study also included an examination of student achievement relative to the teacher's years of experience. Teachers were categorized into five year increments of experience with "twenty or more" representing the highest category. Statistical analysis revealed that there was no correlation between student achievement increase and experience, except in the most senior category—namely, "twenty or more years." The other groups scored at the same level, which demonstrates that *only after many years of experience is there a correlation with higher student achievement.*

In 2010, there was another review of student achievement compared with years of teaching experience within Alberta. Some of these teachers were hired to the province from other provinces, but their familiarity with the provincial curriculum and standards for thirteen-year-old students was lacking. During the years 2005–2010, the percentage of teachers with less than five years of experience increased each year, rising from 26 percent to 41 percent, and decreased annually for teachers with more than twenty years, dropping from 29 percent to 21 percent.

When the results were analyzed, Alberta's achievement scores from the 2011 TIMSS tests were the lowest in their history for grades 4 and 8 students in mathematics. The international test (PISA 2009) in mathematics confirmed the decline, as did Alberta's achievement on the Pan-Canadian Assessment Program (PCAP) in 2010.

In reading, compared to the 2006 PIRLS, Alberta's international ranking slipped from first down to seventh because Alberta's reading score had declined by a statistically significant 12 points. Alberta was the only region that experienced such a significant decrease among the five Canadian provinces that participated in both 2006 and 2011 tests.

We concluded that the decline was due to the fact that there was a significant influx of new teachers into Alberta's schools, combined with a substantial decline in teachers with more than twenty years of experience, resulting in a significant decline in student achievement. Alberta's experience illustrates why the current practice of providing teachers with incremental salary increases during the first five to ten years is inappropriate. Experience does not provide a statistical increase in effectiveness until one has taught much longer. Therefore, a different model for providing teachers with a pay bonus is required.

It is noteworthy that there is no research supporting the merits of the current system. Why do we persist in funding a system that is not providing a return on investment? *Is it possible we are so enslaved to tradition that facts no longer guide our reasoning and logic our decision-making?* Is Bill Gates insightful when he says that education reform is more difficult than eradicating polio, malaria, or tuberculosis? Is the alternative worrisome to unions because value regarding job performance will be assessed based on student outcomes?

With the evidence now available, it is indefensible to continue using the pay grid approach built on certification and years of experience. Jensen and Reichl (2011) get to the nub of the issue: "The implication is that all teachers with the same experience *are paid as though they are equally effective and improve at the same rate.*" It is time to challenge this nonsensical practice, which has been employed for decades.

As long as this practice persists, the system will be more focused on a special-interest group that is intended to serve rather than on the group to be served—namely, the students. Perpetuating the status quo demonstrates we are more interested in currying the favor of a politically powerful employee than we are the client. This, in turn, demonstrates the self-centeredness of our politicians who seek reelection by pandering.

Union opposition toward pay-for-performance programs is fierce and the more intense their opposition the more clearheaded and wise we need our politicians to be. At some point, all of them are likely forced to make a choice: *Will they align with a group that is likely strong enough to elect them, or will they work for the student who is essentially defenseless and certainly incapable of delivering votes on Election Day?* It takes political courage to change course and head in a different direction. More than anything, politicians must respond to the issue that current pay schemes for teachers are inconsequential and outdated.

How does a politician overcome this "catch-22" situation? In a word, it is through transparency. In a political world where the fifteen-second soundbite is so dominant in our media, hard work is required to provide a rationale for political positions. Like a crown prosecutor in the court of law, the philosophical case for coming to a conclusion must be carefully outlined for the jury. Diligent preparation and hard work is required to educate the public so that it looks beyond the opposition of a special interest group.

The politically safe approach used too frequently is to listen only to the employees and their representatives without acquiring an understanding of what lies beneath the surface of their argument. Being knowledgeable requires a lot of data-digging and asking difficult questions. Helping others become knowledgeable requires hard work and risk taking. *More than anything, it requires politicians to begin the public discussion and courageously demonstrate that (as was once written on Starbucks coffee cups) "On the battlefield of ideas, winning requires moving toward the sound of the guns."*

Those guns are now sounding across America and require the engagement of politicians so that the informed voices of parents, public, and media bring pressure for reform. There must be a choir of harmonious voices wanting schools to improve in providing educational services where all students benefit from high standards in both what they learn and who is providing instruction. Smarick (2014) provides a warning:

[The shifting winds now blow with the] exodus of reform-oriented state chiefs. The Race-to-the-Top era made state leaders of prominent reform figures. . . . They led efforts to create next-generation account-ability systems, overhaul tenure and educator evaluation, expand choice, toughen content standards, improve assessments, and more. . . . But that tide is receding. Huge questions are left about reform in these states and others. Though some great chiefs are likely to stay, expect more departures in the months ahead.

The power of teachers' unions should never be underestimated and cannot be overestimated. They exist to serve their members and, contrary to their public utterance, not in pursuit of what may be best for students. The struggle for control of schools is illustrated by the 2012 teachers' strike in Chicago. The *Daily Beast* reported that Rahm Emanuel, newly elected mayor of Chicago, locked horns with the city's union and stated that his predecessor, Richard M. Daley, had caved in to the teachers' union and that the education system was a mess, resulting in students getting "the shaft" (Warren 2012).

Emanuel's blunt assessment of outcomes from teacher negotiations describes an underlying issue in this book. Exactly who is the system serving? Those with a vested interest in the system adamantly state that they and the system are there to serve students. The mayor's curt assess-ment that students get *the shaft* implies that he and others outside the system see a very different agenda at work. Service providers within the educational system are committed to meeting their own needs first and foremost.

Introducing reform into the education system is always a "tough sell." Recently departed U.S. secretary of education Arne Duncan was the ap-pointed leader driving reform to have student achievement comprise part of the teacher's evaluation. His effort included support for paying teachers considerably more than at present *when their results warrant doing so.* Mak (2012) reports:

Education Secretary Arne Duncan said that the starting salaries of teachers should double, up to $65,000 a year, and that excellent teach-ers should be able to make up to $150,000. "I've been very radical on this. I think that young teachers, we should double their salaries [to] $60,000, $65,000. I think that great teachers should be able to make $130,000, $140,000, $150,000—pick a number," said Duncan on MSNBC's "Morning Joe." Duncan said teachers have too often been the target for criticisms about the education system. "We have beaten down educators. We have to elevate the profession, strengthen the profession. Great teachers, great principals make a huge difference in our nation's children," said the education secretary.

Teachers may have appreciated the tenor of his comments in 2012; however, the warm and fuzzy feelings did not last long before icy winds blew. Two years later, teachers demanded his resignation as he continued to promote *paying teachers what they were worth based on their evaluation ratings* (Bidwell 2014).

> Accusing Education Secretary Arne Duncan of undermining public education for reform efforts they disagree with, the union representing millions of public school teachers is asking the top official to shape up or ship out.
>
> The American Federation of Teachers joined its sister union—the National Education Association—in taking a strong stance against the secretary. While the NEA called for Duncan's immediate resignation, the AFT opted to ask for a "Secretary Improvement Plan." And if the secretary does not improve, he would be asked to resign.
>
> The vote represents the union members saying "enough is enough," AFT President Randi Weingarten said in a release. . . . "Teachers are evaluated and their future livelihoods are linked to that," Weingarten said. "And when they fall short, they should have a chance to improve. And that's what this special order represents."

The disrespectful behavior demonstrated by this union's comments about Secretary Duncan is not an atypical example of how they adopt efforts to intimidate. More disturbing is the statement attributed to Weingarten when she says, "And when they [teachers] fall short, they should have a chance to improve. And that's what this special order represents." Of course people should have opportunity to improve; however, the education system does not have a reputation for calling "a spade a spade." Standards are too lax and too many students are subjected to unfair educational opportunity because of poor teaching.

The impetus to ensure that teaching standards are high comes from the highest office in the nation. In a *New York Times* article from March 1, 2010, headlined "Obama Backs Rewarding Districts That Police Failing Schools," President Obama, speaking to the U.S. Chamber of Commerce, stated, "Our kids get only one chance at an education and we need to get it right." The reporter also made it clear that the president "favored federal rewards for local school districts that fire underperforming teachers and close failing schools, saying educators needed to be held accountable when they failed to fix chronically troubled classrooms and curb the student dropout rate."

Fortunately, some in the media are now beginning to educate the public and to provide for much greater transparency in the school system so that an informed public can influence developments in the school. *Waiting for "Superman"*, a pro-education reform documentary, indicated that one out of every fifty-seven doctors loses his or her license to practice medicine; one out of every ninety-seven lawyers loses their license to practice law; and in many major cities, only one out of one thousand teachers is fired for performance-related reasons.

Newspapers now routinely investigate the issue, and their findings are summarized on the Teachers Union Exposed website:

- The *New York Daily News* reports that "over the past three years [2007–2010], just 88 out of some 80,000 (New York) city schoolteachers have lost their jobs for poor performance." (Approximately 0.1 percent)
- The Albany *Times Union* looked at what was going on outside New York City and discovered that of 132,000 teachers; only 32 were fired for any reason between 2006 and 2011. (Approximately 0.02 percent)
- In Chicago, *Newsweek* reported that only 0.1 percent of teachers were dismissed for performance-related reasons between 2005 and 2008. This is a school district that has by any measure failed its students—only 28.5 percent of eleventh graders met or exceeded expectations on that state's standardized tests. (The problem is worse than it seems because there are two Chicagos: north and south. In the north neighborhoods like Lincoln Park are found some of the highest performing schools. So how bad are the schools in the south? The averages make Chicago look bad, but the bad is far worse than the average.)
- The *Los Angeles Times* in 2009 reported that, in a school district where the graduation rate in 2003 was just 51 percent, between 1995 and 2005, only 112 Los Angeles tenured teachers faced termination—eleven per year—out of 43,000. (Approximately 0.03 percent)
- In ten years, only about forty-seven out of one hundred thousand teachers were actually terminated from New Jersey's schools. (Approximately 0.05 percent)

- In any given year in Florida, scholar Richard Kahlenberg wrote, the involuntary dismissal rate for teachers was an abysmally low 0.05 percent, "compared with 7.9 percent in the Florida workforce as a whole."
- In Dallas, even when unofficial pressures to resign are factored in, only 0.78 percent of tenured teachers are terminated.
- Out of Tucson, Arizona's 2,300 tenured teachers, only seven have been fired for classroom behavior in the past five years. (Approximately 0.3 percent)
- Des Moines, Iowa, a school district with almost three thousand teachers, has fired just two for poor performance in five years. (Approximately 0.07 percent)

The Race to the Top American initiative and its emphasis on Common Core standards has captured media attention. Anderson (2013), who writes for the *New York Times*, reported on how teachers are graded, while working in a new culture where evaluations are intended to "provide meaningful feedback and, critically, to weed out weak performers."

For example, in Florida, roughly 100 percent of teachers were deemed effective or highly effective in recent evaluations. Incredibly, teacher evaluations in 2011 typically involved a single observation of about twenty minutes. In Tennessee, 98 percent of teachers were judged to be "at expectations." In Michigan, 98 percent of teachers were rated "effective" or better. An official with the National Council on Teacher Quality conceded in an interview, "There are some alarm bells going off. . . . There's a real culture shift that has to occur and there's a lot of evidence that that hasn't occurred yet."

What is the cultural shift that must happen? Even though teacher evaluations are partly contingent on student test scores, they are mostly focused on principals' assessments acquired through their own observations of teachers. There is a need to abandon a culture where almost all teachers are considered *above average.* We have already pointed out that teacher preparation programs enlist the lower levels of high school graduates seeking to enter post-secondary education. Yet in these programs more students receive "A's" than those in other departments. Simply stated, *standards in education are too low.*

Anderson (2013) points out that this problem of low standards is exacerbated by the involvement of evaluators "who generally are not detached managerial types and can be loath to give teachers low marks."

Education is strengthened by having relational people working with students: it is weakened by requiring these well-intentioned people to "bell the cat" of mediocre colleagues. This emphasis on relationships is why there is not a substantial increase in the percentage of teachers who are removed from the classroom. This may also be why Florida's principals can write their teachers' evaluations based on one twenty-minute observation.

When Anderson informed Grover J. Whitehurst, director of the Brown Center on Education Policy at the Brookings Institution, that very few teachers were deemed "ineffective," he responded, "It would be an unusual profession that at least 5 percent are not deemed ineffective." Evaluating and developing talent is the most important management function in the educational system, whether it is occurring in the classroom with students by their teachers or with teachers by their principals. However, *low standards are endemic in the educational system even though we claim that education is vital for our nation's future well-being.*

Mellon (2010) explores the problem of low standards when evaluating teachers and asks why, in the past, teachers were rarely let go because of poor classroom performance? In an interview with Houston superintendent Terry Grier, who has run nine school districts over twenty-five years, Grier theorizes, "I think some principals accept mediocrity because they don't want to go through the battle with the teachers union or through the process of aggressively recruiting others." *There is a need to apply pressure on those who lack the courage to combat mediocrity.*

Despite the personal attack on Secretary Duncan by Weingarten's union, Mak concludes the report with an observation regarding the union's *conditional support* for Common Core:

> The union also reaffirmed its support of the Common Core State Standards at its national convention in Los Angeles, on the condition of increased monitoring of the standards' implementation and the adoption of a two-year moratorium on the high-stakes consequences of the aligned assessments. Union members voted to adopt the Common Core resolution after a more than 40-minute floor debate, which Weingarten deemed one of the longest she's witnessed. The resolution says the union is "deeply disappointed" with how the standards have been implemented, and feels state leaders have not listened to educators during the process.

Incredibly, in this union meeting, Common Core, despite being the most transformational initiative to surface in American education, received only a forty-minute discussion. The educators did not require much time to repeat their support for Common Core; however, as union members they likely required this time to debate its attachments to common assessment, performance evaluations, and pay.

Facing such pressure from teachers, Secretary Duncan did some backtracking in 2014; according to *U.S. News & World Report*, "Education Secretary Arne Duncan said Thursday that states can apply for extra time before tying teacher evaluations to student test scores, and called for a reduction of over-testing" (Bidwell 2014). NCLB requires all students in grades 3–8 and one grade in high school to be tested annually. Did the call "for a reduction of over-testing" apply to this standard? Bidwell's reporting goes on to say:

> Marc Tucker, president and chief executive officer of the National Center on Education and the Economy, argues in a paper released Thursday that there are several measures to reform the nation's accountability model—essentially a complete overhaul that includes reducing test-taking in schools and creating a career ladder for teachers, among other suggestions. . . . Rather than a sweeping, yearly standardized test, Tucker argues students should be tested on a large scale just three times in their academic careers: at the end of fourth grade, at the end of middle school and at the end of the sophomore year of high school. Additionally, Tucker says schools should use cheaper, multiple-choice assessments to test a sample of students (with an over-sampling of vulnerable students) in second and sixth grade. Those "off-year" tests would cover English and math, as well as science in sixth grade, while the three large-scale tests would cover the entire curriculum, such as science, American and world history, economics, music, the arts, engineering and physical fitness. Notably, though, Tucker proposes that these tests be used to hold students and schools accountable—not teachers. The data would be used to identify schools that might be in trouble, and to send help to investigate and make improvement suggestions. Tucker has also argued that the entire idea of evaluating teachers is illogical.

Definitely Tucker's proposal, as he claims, would be a "complete overhaul," because it will return to the *old-fashioned way of holding students accountable for learning while releasing teachers from their accountability.* Teachers have occupied the pedestal since the beginning of school, which Tucker wants to see happen again. Student assessments once every three years make it impossible to link student achievement to their teacher, just as was said to Tim Pawlenty, governor of Minnesota, several years ago. Secretary Duncan must now hold firm and see that fairness to students "wins the day" and allows them to take their rightful place on the educational pedestal.

Incorporating annual assessment removes the obstacle for incorporating a teacher's performance evaluation into their pay. This step is a transformational issue in education. Such a requirement may be intuitive to all those working within the private sector and it may come as a surprise that teachers are not paid according to how well they perform in their role. Race to the Top is changing the school system's perspective by requiring that teachers' evaluations be based, in part, on how well students learn from their teachers.

Common Core is the genesis for this new approach because it places all educators onto the same field of play. Using the same standards across the nation provides a consistent yardstick for determining whether students receive high-quality teaching as measured by high-quality tests used across all regions. Common Core must be linked with common assessment in order for common measurement to occur. These commonalities are necessary for ensuring that all students receive fair opportunity to excel.

The time has come when teachers together with their administrators are held accountable for how well their students are taught. Everyone performs better when some pressure is evident and based on how well they fulfill the requirements of employment. Remuneration should have some portion that is at risk and that rewards workers according to the results of their efforts.

The key points made in this chapter are as follows:

- Initially, teachers supported Common Core, but their support is eroding because of the link with common assessment, which, in turn, is linked with performance evaluations culminating in a linkage with pay.
- In the 2016 presidential election, a decision by the Republican candidate to withdraw support for Common Core would free the Democratic candidate from declaring support for the pay-for-performance component.

- Teachers are all paid the same salary but receive unjustified bonuses for years of experience and additional certification.
- Early merit pay programs in education failed because they were too subjective and not focused on student outcomes.
- Teacher performance evaluations are flawed because they did not consider student achievement.
- Empirical evidence does not substantiate paying teachers for gaining experience in their initial years of teaching, nor for acquiring additional certification other than for specializing in mathematics and sciences.
- Legal costs associated with firing poor teachers were so prohibitive that terminations were infrequent.
- Extrinsic motivation is applicable to those working in the educational sector.

TEN

Common Sense about Continuous Pass

An earlier chapter demonstrates ongoing significant disparities on test results between U.S. states. National results on international tests also demonstrate that America's students remain mired well below many nations we would consider as peers. For too many decades the American school system has allowed low standards to prevail in classrooms by following a process of allowing weak students to progress without demonstrating standards of learning. This process, known as social promotion or continuous pass, insidiously diminished accountability for both the educators and their students.

In a nutshell, social promotion is the practice of advancing students to the next grade level even when they have not fully met the academic requirements in their present year of school. Rather than grouping students by academic success, keeping students with their age peers is the primary objective. "The argument for social promotion rests primarily upon the claim that students kept behind end up worse off academically and emotionally than those socially promoted" (Zwaagstra and Clifton 2009).

Another chapter summarizes the considerable evidence regarding how inconsistent teachers' classroom marks can be and that these inconsistencies are skewed upward resulting in grade inflation. In other words, information provided to parents consistently reports student achievement at a higher level than what is factual. Teachers, while well intentioned, are fallible humans susceptible to bias, which, in the school system, usually revolves around issues of compliant behaviors. Cooperation with teachers' expectations produces a more favorable attitude toward students when their work is assessed.

Grade inflation in education knows no borders. Earlier, we referenced a UK study by Durham University concluding that an "A" grade in 2009 was the equivalent to a "C" grade in the 1980s. The slippery slope endured for three decades and people wonder why students appear less prepared for their world of work. According to the *Daily Telegraph*, this trend goes hand in hand with the "all must have prizes" ethos that has dominated education for decades, to the detriment of academic excellence. The newspaper's summative statement was that "these are the effects of grade inflation that has become endemic in public examinations."

The educational system today is not the same as it was for our grandparents or for the parents who are currently raising children. Rules such as entry date have remained the same, but the practices in our schools have changed. For example, when educators faced universal participation, they initially failed students who fell behind their grade placement. An article in one of Canada's national newspapers, the *Globe and Mail* (June 9, 2007), touched on this issue. Writing about the experiences of the Edmonton public school district, the article stated:

> The realization crept up on Edmonton school administrators and shocked them to the core: One in five children was failing Grade 1. It was the early 1980s and officials learned of the high retention rate by chance through a testing program that found that about 20 per cent of pupils, many of them boys whose birthdays fell just before the enrolment cutoff, were in their second year of Grade 1.

Failing students certainly was common in those days, and birth month, especially for boys, was a significant factor. The newspaper article went on to explain that by 2007, across Canada, holding children back has become increasingly rare. *Instead, children who failed to meet minimum grade standards usually moved ahead with their peers. This is the practice we refer to as social promotion.*

This practice arose out of well-intentioned compassion for children who were thought to suffer from poor self-esteem if they were held back. Studies seemed to suggest that students experienced more success in school if they remained with age-level peers. The article indicated, however, that among teachers there is dissent about the merits of social promotion, with some seeing the practice as ineffective in addressing gaps in learning (Dueck 2013).

During focus groups to acquire anecdotal evidence, a teacher provided a perspective regarding the school's accountability for learners pushed ahead while struggling to keep pace when she said, "We do the children and ourselves a great disservice as a society to promote these kids through the system because we're embarrassed at their failures and lack of progress." Passing a student on to another teacher in the next grade is too easy a solution in an environment prone toward social promotion.

Another grade 1 teacher expressed her opinion by referencing a student who did not want to come to school because he knew he was not as successful as his friends. The teacher went on to say the boy was born near the end of the registration window. Therefore, she felt a moral imperative draw her toward this struggling student because she knew that stronger students in the classroom bond socially and shun weaker students. She expressed a deep, personal need to make sure that the needs of lower-end students were not forgotten because this is the most important need in teaching.

Thus she acknowledged feeling pressure to *adapt the curriculum* to meet students' needs, that is, to adjust downward her expectations for the curriculum, classroom activities, and homework. Put in the colloquial language of the day, it was her responsibility to "dumb down" the learning environment to a point where the slowest students experienced success. Educators usually find the term "dumb down" offensive, and understandably so. Its use promotes a negative perception of teaching.

Inevitably, the educational needs of weak students become the teachers' primary focus because having all students meet minimum requirements is the educators' moral imperative. *Unfortunately, the educational needs of our brightest and best students become secondary to the needs of those benefiting from the moral imperative.* When factoring the impact of grade inflation in a setting using social promotion, where the needs of weak students have primary focus, the marks given to stronger students too frequently are higher than what is warranted. *Parents of these stronger students are lulled into a false sense that their child is excelling.*

Teachers in the focus group referenced another pressure related to social promotion. They indicated an understanding that parents feel peer pressure regarding the progress of their child. In fact, teachers feel pressure from many parents who want more and faster learning to occur. If parents hear bad news about their child's lack of success, they take it personally and seek to attribute blame. Sometimes parents take out their frustration on their children using inappropriate verbal comments or physical actions, thereby making the problem more acute.

Consequently, teachers are reluctant to be the bearers of bad news. Parents then remain ignorant of the situation and the relationship between the teacher, the school, and the parents remains cordial and artificially productive. If the issue was simply one of producing a consumer product or of providing a nonessential service, the lack of transparency would still be wrong, but the consequences would not be so tragic. The lines of communication between teachers and parents need to be open and characterized by informed integrity. Why? One superintendent explained it this way: "We need to change the system because the system is supposed to be here to serve the kids."

Another administrator stated that he felt there were few in the public, including parents, who would be able to understand that many children were functioning below grade level. He was referencing a problem he saw among parents of middle school students, and his concern was that they would soon be arriving at the high school where he was the principal, and where teachers placed greater emphasis on teaching prescribed curricular content than on adapting content for significant variations in student ability.

Unless a school system has undertaken the arduous process of articulating standards for its curriculum, a relatively common approach in secondary schools is to segregate students by ability and then apply the Bell Curve to assess academic progress. Unfortunately, this assessment practice only serves to mislead everyone regarding the true achievement of the learner and, again, *hide from public view a true description of learning.*

One parent in a focus group related a poignant story of how the social promotion system almost led to a disastrous result for her son. "For many years," she said, "we were misled into believing our son was doing fine in school. When he was in grade 9 his classroom teacher told us he was functioning at a grade 5 level." The parent then explained that it took her some time to get over the shock of this revelation, but when she did she spared no expense in acquiring costly compensatory programming for him to bring him back to his proper grade level.

Once he enrolled in university and experienced success there, she felt sufficiently confident about what had happened and what needed to be done to share her experience with other parents. Her goal, she said, was "to ensure parents would be sensitized to the lack of transparency that is in the school system."

Many school administrators today willingly acknowledge that their school's efforts to meet the moral imperative are disadvantaging stronger students. In their focus group, these educational leaders described situations where the stronger students were "spinning their wheels" because teachers are so focused on meeting the needs of weaker students that they did not have the time and the energy to address the needs of stronger students. This led to comments that students experiencing behavioral problems were bright students who were not having their needs met. In the colorful language of one principal's metaphor, *"Stronger students are nails that stand up; teachers hammer them down, resulting in rebellion."*

School district trustees were the last group to address this issue, and they, too, expressed a similar perspective on the impact social promotion was having on the academically stronger students. It was their perception that these students were not getting the attention they required to stretch and challenge them in accordance with their ability. However, while they were on the topic of social promotion, some trustees digressed to make the point that they were hearing disgruntled voices in the community who wanted the school district to discontinue its practice of promoting students who fell even further behind their age peers. *The trustees concurred a newer attitude was emerging that this ongoing practice should not continue.*

The trustees were sympathetic about the problems a change like this would bring and they recognized that teachers, "Don't like to hold kids back" and, therefore, stopping this long-time practice was going to require massive reeducation in the system. These trustees, then, could easily see how a current emphasis on the weak students was a deterrent to academically strong students who would have achieved their potential if the teachers had provided them with their "fair share" of time, resources, and support.

The anecdotal comments from these focus groups are in keeping with survey results of a more general population reported in *Education Week* in 2004:

> Public opinion is strongly behind ending social promotion. About three-quarters of parents, and more than 80 percent of teachers and employers, think it is worse for a child struggling in school to be pro-

moted to the next grade than to be held back. Only 24 percent of parents and 15 percent of teachers think it is worse for a student to have to repeat a grade. A full 87 percent of parents surveyed said they would approve of policies that require students to pass a test to be promoted, even if it meant their child would be left back. (Editorial Projects in Education Research Center 2004)

The problem of merely passing students along without achieving standards is facilitated by a culture in which a career in teaching qualifies as a job-for-life. Rarely is a teacher's employment terminated for poor performance; yet, the data demonstrates significant differences in student achievement based on teacher talent. The profession suffers from low standards in its evaluation process and/or from lack of courage by teacher evaluators. In this culture of low expectations, many students are disadvantaged in their education, which also communicates a contradictory message about how we value our children and the education each receives.

A work environment, in which all are deemed to have passed, degrades the quality of the product, which, in education, is a well-educated student—not just some of them or most of them but *all* of them. If the school system does not have high standards for its teachers, they may not be committed to setting high expectations for their students. The ripple effect for the worker can be evident in the product. In this regard, the effects of teacher tenure and inflated performance evaluations influence negatively the expectations teachers have for the nation's students.

We have also demonstrated that aspiring teachers journeying through their university pre-service programs are recipients of course marks that are well beyond the range of any other program. In other words, preservice students are accustomed to receiving highly inflated marks during their university training and, therefore, too readily accept lower standards from their students—standards they themselves experienced in the system. *It is difficult to demand excellence when excellence was not demanded of you.*

At the same time, the international McKinsey report on *How the World's Best Performing School Systems Come Out On Top* quoted a representative of the U.S. Commission On Skills of the American Workforce, who said, "We are now recruiting our teachers from the bottom third of high school graduates going to college." Students going into teaching are not the top academic students; yet they are graduating from their training programs with the highest marks. Some people might argue that universities' education faculties are providing such a stellar education for their students that they are being transformed into exceptional practitioners.

TEACHERS' STRONG RELATIONAL QUALITIES ARE A WEAKNESS FOR EVALUATING ACHIEVEMENT

While teachers work in a world where their own performance is assessed against standards that are too low, they possess a relational talent deemed necessary for effective teaching. They work with a wide range of students and must understand all personality types. Ability to deal with occasional bizarre behavior requires someone who loves and understands children. *But in their role as assessors of student achievement, teachers' strength in building relationships becomes their weakness in evaluating student learning.* Strengths frequently have an *Achilles' heel*, and providing difficult evaluations may lead to conflict, which is troublesome for many teachers.

Every occupation experiences a wide range of employee talent, and teaching is not without its share of poor performers. Teachers, perhaps unwittingly, are able to cover up their low application of standards in their classrooms by the well-documented fact that grade inflation is rampant in our schools. Parents are delighted to hear how well their children are doing in school because their report cards illustrate such high levels of achievement.

One principal noted his observations with a teacher whom he assessed as being just above the competent threshold. The teacher had strong parental support because students received high marks during the year they were in his class. The principal's concerns with this teacher arose when students did not receive high marks in the following years when receiving instruction from other teachers.

Unfortunately, there is a day of reckoning when students write exit examinations in grade 12 or enter university in departments other than education. This was the case in the province of Ontario, where students registering for university with an "A" average in grade 12 escalated from 18 percent in 1995 to 40 percent in 2007 (Dueck 2013). Obviously student achievement was really improving, and the school system should be the recipient of high honors for its success. However, university instructors from twenty-two institutions across that province reported an entirely different story in a 2009 survey in the Ontario Confederation of University Faculty publication.

Instructors responded to the question, "Thinking about your own experience over the last three years, how well prepared do you believe first year students are for your class?" Only 2 percent indicated that students were "better prepared," while 65 percent of opinionated responses indicated that students were actually "less prepared." On November 29, 2011, a university dean commented, "As admissions become more difficult and competitive, each school in Ontario tends to say let's give our students a leg up by giving them higher grades. . . . There's an arms race of A's going on."

While Ontario universities were loath to admit it publicly for fear of creating controversy, there was a significant disconnect between the school system and post-secondary institutions regarding the quality of education received. Such fraudulent behavior by grade 12 teachers is fooling the student and his or her parents into thinking that their child is achieving high standards. Even worse, such a misrepresentation to the public is an insult to the educational system and provides clear evidence that accountability is lacking.

It is against this backdrop of low standards that we examine the phenomenon of *social promotion,* or *continuous pass,* for students. Elementary schools are particularly complex places because learning is so irregular. In other words, students' maturation impacts their rates of learning and their rates of learning vary between subjects. It is possible that a child in his or her fifth year in school is demonstrating learning in reading that is consistent with the grade 6 curriculum, but when it comes to mathematics, they may be consistent with the grade 3 curriculum. Therefore, a heterogeneous class identified with one grade of students is actually comprised of many grade levels of achievement.

SOCIAL PROMOTION REDUCES ACCOUNTABILITY

Weaknesses in teachers' knowledge and skills in using student assessment and differentiating instruction for student learning contribute toward an erroneous perception regarding how children progress through our school system. The critical balance is disturbed between the competing approaches of social promotion and the strict adherence required to meet grade standards. The former approach recognizes value in having students placed with age appropriate peers, whereas the latter produces pass/fail accountability and attention to standards.

Schools originally emphasized student progress based on meeting grade-level standards; however, difficulties arose when school attendance became mandatory to age sixteen and older. Too many students found it difficult to maintain pace with the grade curriculum and were failed. Many students were actually failed on more than one occasion while they pursued graduation requirements.

One principal explained how difficult it was to deal with a student in a K–7 elementary school who arrived driving his own vehicle. Another administrator spoke about high school athletic teams including twenty-two-year-old players. The social problems associated with this pass/fail approach while expecting graduation for all students contributed to a dramatic rise in today's extensive use of social promotion. Many educators chose to adapt the curriculum and promote students with age-appropriate peers.

Adopting a social promotion approach for progressing students through the educational system created a different set of problems for our schools. A principal explained his concern about low achievement with his middle school students. After testing reading levels with the entire population of grade 9 students, he found that almost one-half were functioning at more than two grade levels below grade placement. Students were just being pushed through the school's program without appropriate intervention. *Students were being taught English, but no one was teaching them to read it.*

There is a delicate balance when working with young students between using pass/fail accountability and social promotion. Too many students now are merely being pushed through the school system because social promotion is so dominant. *Schools have lost their zeal for ensuring that students meet grade-level standards.* The evidence is most acute in our universities, which provide extensive remediation and preparation courses for students exiting high schools. When working on the American Common Core standards in the Race to the Top initiative, educational leaders indicated that the average high school graduate in some states was achieving at grade 10 standards.

The problem is so significant in American schools that the forty-five participating states were required to sign commitments that all students, beginning in grade 3, would be tested several times a year; post-secondary institutions would accept students' graduation marks; and institutions would abort the current practice of operating remedial courses to compensate for skill deficiencies in students entering their programs. *In other words, there is a concerted effort to move Common Core and common assessment closer to a practice characterized by integrity.*

The imbalance given to social promotion has wrought enough damage to America's school system. Although a few students with special needs are unable to progress based on achievement, and therefore require social promotion, this is not true for the rest of the student population. However, the current situation is not unlike the gaming-the-system situation at the turn of this century, when approximately 20 percent of American students were excused from system-wide tests because there was a concern that the tests were too difficult.

No Child Left Behind legislation rectified this problem so that participation rates now exceed 95 percent. Government officials are obligated to intervene and rectify indefensible practices employed by personnel attempting to "game" the system. A mentality of "pushing them through" is too dominant over one where the school system feels pressure to take action and apply emergency measures for ensuring that more students succeed.

The "continuous pass" orientation had a significant effect on the educational system. Cunningham and Owens (1976) provided an appropriate summary about social promotion: "Social promotion is accomplishing what it was intended to do; it is relieving the various grades of over-age, floundering students. If we are to help these potential failures we must devise new educational systems." According to the *U.S. National Center for Education Statistics* (2006), in 2004, only 9.6 percent of youth ages 16–19 had been retained in a grade at some point. This represented a decrease from 16.1 percent in 1995 (a reduction of 6.5 percentage points or 40 percent).

At the apex of this movement, Thompson and Cunningham (2000) summarized the considerable confusion evident at that time:

> The issue of whether it is better to retain low-performing students in grade or to pass them along with their age-mates has been both hotly disputed and heavily studied for decades. Advocates of retention have maintained that it sends a message to all students that weak effort and poor performance will not be tolerated, and that it gives lagging students an opportunity to get serious and get ready for the next grade.

Opponents have argued that retention discourages students whose motivation and confidence are already shaky, and that promoted students gain an opportunity to advance through the next year's curriculum, while retained students go over the same ground and thus fall farther behind their advancing peers.

Part of the confusion is evident in the last line with the words "retained students go over the same ground." This was poor practice where teachers expected the same pace for all learners. During the school year, relatively little adjustment was made to accommodate the struggling student and, at the conclusion of the year, *they were declared failures*. In other words, they started school the next year at the same place as a year earlier and *repeated* the curriculum. This method for dealing with struggling learners is consistent with the term *fail*, and it is poor practice.

Some schools utilized a different approach, which did not have students "go over the same ground." *They never failed, but they were retained*. As soon as teachers detected that a student was falling behind, individualized programming occurred and the instructional pace for that student was adjusted. Usually falling behind one year in the curriculum took more than one year in school, or they began school already deficient in their intellectual maturation. *In effect, the school was shouldering responsibility for ensuring that this learner experienced success*.

When this student fell more than a year behind peers, the school, in consultation with parents, made a decision to *retain* the student with a younger group. Frequently the additional year of intellectual maturity allowed for a normal pace of learning, but this student did not experience the gaps in instruction or repetitive teaching used in the approach more appropriately labeled "fail." What mattered is that grade-level standards were the key factor in placement decisions.

Social promotion disregarded the poor practice of failing and the more acceptable practice of retaining. Its defining feature is that students remained with age-appropriate peers with an expectation that teaching would be adjusted to accommodate the learner. Intellectual maturation necessary for successful progress could remain a problem.

Thompson and Cunningham provided the following conclusion about the merits of both approaches:

> Overall, neither social promotion nor retention leads to high performance. If the goal is to bring low-performing students up to the higher standards now being asserted across the nation, neither retention nor

social promotion is effective. In different studies, one or the other has
been found to offer an advantage, but neither has been found to offer a
large, lasting advantage, and neither leads to high performance.

This study is significant because it refutes the practice embraced by the majority
of schools that social promotion was a superior alternative to retention. In other
words, greater emphasis should be placed on holding students and educators
accountable for students' academic success. Therefore, assessing student learn-
ing is an important activity within the education system.

Reaction against this policy of social promotion recorded by Public
Agenda, released on February 21, 2001, demonstrated an attitudinal shift
taking place across the American school system:

> The number of teachers who say their own schools practice social pro-
> motion has dropped from 41% to 31% over the last four years, accord-
> ing to a new nationwide survey by nonpartisan, nonprofit Public Agen-
> da. *Reality Check 2001*, which surveys teachers, parents, students, em-
> ployers and college professors on standards in their community, was
> published in today's issue of Education Week. It also shows an increase
> in summer school attendance and more positive attitudes among par-
> ents about standards in public schools.

This report goes on to explain how the change in attitudes regarding use
of social promotion was changing practices in schools. The number of
teachers reporting student attendance in summer school jumped from 28
percent four years earlier to 37 percent. Further, the number of teachers
who said that students now take summer school seriously rose to 53
percent, an increase of ten percentage points since 1998.

A positive spin-off on parental attitudes was also reported, and demonstrates that social promotion was controversial with them. The number
of parents saying that local public schools have higher standards than
local private schools rose from 22 percent in 1998 to 34 percent, while the
number of parents saying private schools have higher standards fell from
42 percent four years ago to 35 percent. Parents are supporting this shift
toward higher standards in public schools.

Debating social promotion versus retention produced a difference of
opinion regarding research methodology. Some researchers, as reported
in a White Paper by the National Association of School Psychologists,
argued that same-grade comparisons are more consistent with the purpose of retention, which is to provide students the opportunity to be

more successful in meeting the academic demands of future grades (Karweit 1999; Lorence 2006).

This White Paper provides a meta-analysis of studies on these educational approaches that reinforces retention as a more productive strategy than social promotion:

> A recent meta-analysis of 207 achievement effects nested in 22 studies published from 1990 to 2007 (Allen, Chen, Willson, & Hughes, 2009) determined that studies that used higher quality controls for selection effects (i.e., pre-retention differences between students selected for retention intervention and promoted peers) resulted in less negative effects for retention. . . . Although retaining students who fail to meet grade level standards has limited empirical support, promoting students to the next grade when they have not mastered the curriculum of their current grade, a practice termed social promotion, is not an educationally sound alternative. For these reasons, the debate over the dichotomy between grade retention and social promotion must be replaced with efforts to identify and disseminate evidence-based practices that promote academic success for students whose academic skills are below grade level standards.

Patricia Hawke (2006) examined results in Florida, which began moving away from its reliance on social promotion as their improvement strategy.

> The findings of the Florida schools' study showed that the performance gain of the retained students in 2002 exceeded that of the socially promoted students in 2001. The improvement gains were moderate in reading, yet significant in mathematics. The results were consistent in both the FCAT and Stanford-9 tests, showing the gains were due to student skill mastery rather than prepping.

Greene and Winters (2011) later provided their perspectives on Florida's reform effort and gave additional support for the use of retention as opposed to automatic promotion:

> Previous studies examined retention based on educator discretion. In a new study we conducted for the Manhattan Institute that avoids the pitfalls of earlier research, we find that holding low-performing students back helps them academically. We examined a policy in Florida that required third-grade students to perform at a certain level on the state's reading test to receive an automatic promotion to fourth grade. Students who performed below the required level and repeated third grade made significantly greater academic progress than similar stu-

dents who were promoted despite their lack of skills. The benefit of being retained grew so that by the end of the second year the retained students entered fifth grade knowing more than the promoted students did leaving fifth grade—this despite the fact that the retained students had not yet been exposed to the fifth grade material.

New York City, another school system working to adopt system accountability for student success, also shifted away from social promotion. McCombs et al. (2009) reported on that city's policy for assisting students who were falling behind:

> The policy places considerable emphasis on identifying struggling students early, providing them with additional instructional time, and continuously monitoring their achievement. Students who have been identified as in need of services at the beginning of the school year (based on their performance on the previous year's assessments, teacher recommendations, or being previously retained in grade) are mandated to receive academic intervention services (AIS) in school. In addition, schools can offer a variety of out-of-school support services, including Saturday school (previously called Saturday Preparatory Academies). Students who fail to score Level 2 or higher on the mathematics or ELA [English Language Arts] assessments administered in the spring are offered several opportunities to meet the promotion standards and can be promoted based on (1) a review of a portfolio of their work in the spring, (2) performance on the summer standardized assessment, (3) a review of a portfolio of their work in August, or (4) an appeal process. Students who do not meet the standards when their portfolios are reviewed in the spring are required to enroll in the Summer Success Academy, which offers additional hours of intensive instruction in mathematics and ELA for several weeks in the summer.

When it came time to report on the results, these authors indicate this school system's success while accepting responsibility for helping their students succeed:

> Scoring at the proficiency level (Level 3 or higher) in NYC schools has increased dramatically, while the percentage of students scoring Level 1 has declined equally dramatically—and this was true across the rest of New York State as well.
>
> Examples:
>
> Mathematics in Grade 7 from 2006 to 2008
>
> • Level 3 (Proficiency): improved by 25 percentage points

- Level 1: declined to 3 percent

English Language Arts in grade 5 from 2006 to 2008

- Proficiency: Improved 17 percentage points

It appears likely that these improvements are related to the set of reforms enacted by the city and state in the NCLB context. We also found no negative effects of retention on students' sense of school belonging or confidence in mathematics and reading over time. The near-term benefits we found hold out the possibility of longer term benefits as well.

The RAND Corporation reviewed the New York City policy's results and concluded:

> Administrators reported that the promotion policy focused the instructional efforts of schools, made parents more concerned about student progress, and provided additional resources to support low-achieving students. Overall, retained students did not report negative socio-emotional effects.

Reviewing this New York study poses an interesting question: How do their students fare in subsequent years? A new report, by the National Center for Education Statistics, compares each state's performance on state tests with their performance on the 2013 National Assessment of Educational Performance—or NAEP. *New York was the only state that reached NAEP's proficiency range for fourth- and eighth-graders in both reading and mathematics.* Undoubtedly, this state's results are highly influenced by New York City, and leadership there—that is, Mayor Bloomberg—contributed positive leadership for that education system.

The underlying point in this research is that much of our educational system adopted social promotion as the dominant strategy for dealing with students experiencing difficulty in achieving more normal academic progress. It was the most common alternative to failing students rather than a better, but more costly, alternative using *early identification* of students who are not meeting grade expectations and the provision of individualized, accelerated instruction utilizing evidence-based instructional practices and frequent progress monitoring.

Other reform strategies were also not considered, including the approach of delaying entrance into the school until a child is more mature. Several European countries, including Finland, wait until children are seven years of age prior to beginning formal learning. Another strategy would be to reduce the age spread in the cohort of students from twelve to six months so disparities in intellectual maturation within a grouping of students are not so significant (Dueck 2013). These alternatives would be more transformational but also more controversial because of the changes required in people's attitudes.

Rather than consider these alternatives, most educators until recently preferred to base their decisions on a flawed methodology in measuring retention, believing that social promotion was at least an improvement. *Doing something was better than doing nothing, even if the something was not helpful.* Believing that the social promotion approach represented a legitimate strategy, educational leaders accepted the approach, believing they were "off the hook." Many actually thought they were demonstrating compassion and responsibility because they assumed the students' needs were being met. At the same time, pressure to perform, which we know is beneficial, was reduced by social promotion.

Whether the terminology is "continuous pass" or "all pass," the social promotion approach remains far too encompassing. There are some students with exceptional needs who are unable to achieve standards, but applying this approach to a large percentage of the student population changes the culture of the educational system. Not only are expectations lowered, but higher achievers also do not have their needs adequately addressed because attention and resources are directed more toward those falling behind their age group (Dueck 2013; Xiang et al. 2011).

LOWERING STUDENT EXPECTATIONS CORRELATES WITH LOW PROFESSIONAL STANDARDS

Choosing an instructional approach that lowered expectations for students was accelerated by several factors. Low standards in our teacher preparation programs attracted our academically weaker high school graduates. Effort is a significant component for achieving academic excellence, and lower-achieving high school graduates may also be characterized by lower levels of motivation. Intellectual capacity is a significant factor in teaching when thinking creatively for planning lessons that inspire learning.

Once accepted into teacher education, aspiring teachers are victimized by participating in a program characterized by lower standards where less work is required to achieve excellence. Then, after gaining employment, teachers' performance in the workplace is evaluated against sufficiently low standards so that everyone retains a satisfactory score and no one loses their job.

These aspects of the educational system demonstrate how it functions in a manner that does not contribute sufficiently to our nation's long-term success. Rather, it contradicts our claim that education is our society's most important profession. Rhetoric by itself is insufficient! To live well we must learn well, and our political leaders must embrace strategies that *demand more from the educational system*, without merely "throwing more money" at it. Their low expectations for the educational system are an impediment to our future capacity to "live well."

FOCUSING TEACHER ATTENTION ON STUDENT ACHIEVEMENT

Ongoing communication with teachers regarding their students' academic success is a powerful method to reduce tendencies toward social promotion. Over many years, my administrative practices incorporated asking teachers to identify the grade level that each student in their class was achieving in language arts and mathematics. After requesting this information countless times and finding that teachers were always able to identify the appropriate grade, even if the child had only been in the class for two months, it is clear that assessing children's learning at the appropriate grade is not a difficult challenge for our teachers.

The question does not have to be more scientific than whether the student is "below," "at," or "above" their grade designation. Responding to this question for both subjects does not require any additional work, and it provides another tracking of student performance from the teacher's perspective for several units of analysis—for example, class, school, district, and state.

The key in this approach is that responses are recorded quarterly to coincide with the distribution of students' report cards. These discussions also trigger partnerships between teachers and administrators regarding how an individual student's academic needs can be addressed as well as needs related to their social and emotional development. One principal, faced with a request from the superintendent to understand why his school repeatedly experienced higher test scores than expected, related how this approach was identified by teachers as providing the greatest impact on student success.

At the conclusion of the school year, summative results from this approach can be recorded on the student's final report card as well as on official records within the system. For example, Edmonton Public Schools, a highly acclaimed school district internationally, provided parents with access to a password-protected portal that summarizes their child's annual assessment for more than a decade. This approach not only provides parents with a summative evaluation of their child's progress but also enhances accountability within its system.

Parents can quickly determine whether their child is succeeding. School administrators can monitor annual progress of their students as determined by the classroom teacher's assessment. School district officials can report to their school board on the state of student achievement in these two core subjects. Standardized test results can be correlated with these teacher assessments to determine anomalous information. Recording the teacher's response to a simple question makes this school district data-rich where students are the beneficiaries.

An attempt to expand this approach to the provincial/state level revealed the fear teachers, and their union, have regarding accountability. The union immediately and aggressively mounted a campaign to halt any attempt to have this information become part of the region's reporting. In other words, *not only was it opposed to reporting results on standardized testing, but it was equally vociferous about the inappropriateness of reporting teachers' assessment of student progress.*

In teacher forums across the region, many vocalized their concern about the additional work required for providing the information. At each forum, as this issue was voiced, a simple experiment quickly dispelled the concern. When the concern regarding time was expressed, the teacher was requested to "think of a specific student in their class but not verbalize his or her name." Within seconds the teacher indicated they had a student in mind. Within seconds they could say whether that student was achieving "at," "above," or "below" grade placement. Workload was not the issue.

These discussions revealed a sad situation in the region. Written policy required teachers to provide parents with the "grade level(s) the child has achieved in relation to the grade levels of the programs of study for language arts and mathematics." Implementation of this policy was haphazard and, apparently, school administrators were not ensuring that parents received this vital information.

These discussions revealed the real issue: fear about whether teachers' assessments would be consistent from one year to the next. Inconsistent grading of student achievement was raising its ugly head. Social promotion was revealing that many students were well behind grade placement. Putting a number down in "black and white" was too threatening for many teachers, who were frightened about being contradicted by a colleague.

The union's agenda was exposed. They wanted teachers' assessments to be trusted without using standardized test results. They did not want a requirement that teachers report this assessment to a data center for further analysis, because the aggregated information—non-student specific—might be accessed by external agencies. Accountability is accompanied with transparency, and these concepts place pressure that may be unwelcome.

The pendulum provides an appropriate metaphor for the ongoing struggle between two educational approaches related to how students progress through the school system. The focus on whether to socially promote or retain students stirs passionate debate, which suggests that the right response is not a rule but a generalization. The extreme ends of the pendulum's swings are not the most appropriate response, indicating a need to consider each student's situation.

The point of this chapter is that social promotion or, as it can also be named, continuous pass, was overused between 1970 and 2000. *In other words, social promotion for students unable to demonstrate grade standards became too automatic.* NCLB produced some necessary pressure to change the mindset in the nation's education system so that all children were not just waived through school.

Introducing common assessments, even when these were conducted at the state level, provided impetus for reassessing whether automatic promotion was the best course of action. The school system must experience a degree of pressure emanating from using ongoing assessments, which raise the *flag of concern* about addressing the needs of students struggling to keep pace. Common Core raises standards across participating states and, when linked with common assessment, applies a greater level of accountability for the school system to adjust classroom instruction and activities to the individual needs of students.

Some people want to debate whether assessment should be based on standardized testing or teachers' perceptions of student progress. Such a debate is not appropriate because assessment should comprise both forms. This book promotes a theme that standardized assessments are a necessary part of any assessment program. At the same time, pressure from a measurement system using standardized tests should be supplemented by incorporating teacher assessments through reporting a student's grade level of achievement. This summative information, based on the teachers' perception, should be reported to parents annually.

The key points made in this chapter are as follows:

- Low expectations of teachers contribute to their low expectations of students.
- Teacher preparation programs suffer from abnormal levels of grade inflation.
- Teachers' capacity to build relationships with students presents a weakness in assessing their achievement.
- Grade inflation distorts information to parents regarding their child's progress.
- Social promotion dilutes adherence to grade-level standards.
- Heterogeneous classes contain students achieving at many different grade levels.
- Grade retention may not be the preferred strategy for dealing with students, but it is a more productive strategy than social promotion.
- Discussions between teachers and school administrators regarding students' grade level of achievement increases the potential for personalized learning and decreases the practice of social promotion.

ELEVEN

Common Sense Is Prevailing

An overwhelming majority of governors purposed to establish Common Core standards across their states as a means of raising academic expectations for their students. Early educator support for Common Core coupled with an ambivalent media has changed since the 2012 American elections. The focus on this initiative is increasing to the extent that tensions are building for the 2016 elections. Many educators are abandoning their support because testing student achievement relative to these common standards becomes part of their performance evaluations. In turn, these evaluations will comprise part of their remuneration package.

Faced with the reality that consequences of their performance in the classroom will finally mean something, teachers and their unions want common assessment scuttled. The absence of data on individual student outcomes negates differentiated evaluations based on student success. Teachers are comfortable with receiving bonuses for getting older and acquiring additional certification, but moving to performance on the job is too threatening. Teacher opposition to this threat is consolidating through their unions, who feel a sense of urgency in acquiring support from the people they want to represent.

TEACHERS' UNIONS' STAKE IN COMMON CORE

Teachers' unions are controversial in educational politics, and an aspect of the controversy they generate is whether they are a stumbling block to reform or advocates for better schools and better teachers. Public attitudes regarding this differing perspective are shifting. Peterson et al. (2012) asked Americans, "Do you think teachers' unions have a generally positive effect on schools, or do you think they have a generally negative effect?"

While 41 percent of the public selected the neutral position, those with a positive view of unions dropped to 22 percent in 2012 from 29 percent in 2011. The survey's most striking finding was "that 58% of teachers took a positive view of unions in 2011, and only 43% do in 2012. The number of teachers holding negative views of unions nearly doubled to 32% from 17%."

The commitment to unionism in the United States also reflects differing perceptions teachers have on one of the more contentious issues in the world of education today, namely pay-for-performance based, in part, on standardized test scores. Farkas et al. (2003) report:

> On virtually every proposal for rewarding teachers differentially, southern teachers are more open compared with teachers in other regions throughout the country. Even when it comes to using standardized test scores to determine teachers' pay—the proposal that was least popular among all teachers—half (50%) of southern teachers favor it, compared with 36% in the Midwest, 34% in the West and just 26% in the Northeast.

Teachers' unions may have a cause célèbre in opposing pay-for-performance with those teachers living in unionized regions and where population density has a larger worker force.

Teachers' unions are closely aligned with the Democratic Party. According to the Teachers Union Exposed website:

> There is no doubt where the union's political allegiances lie, even if they don't correspond to their members' political beliefs. Between 1990 and 2008, ninety-three percent of donations made by National Education Association political action committees and individual officers went to Democrats, according to the Center for Responsive Politics. But the NEA admits that only 45 percent of public school teachers are Democrats.

The Center for Responsive Politics website provides additional specificity in its reporting on campaign contributions by the two American (AFT/NEA) teachers' unions:

> The industry is overwhelmingly liberal, even more than the average union category. The share of teachers unions' contributions going to

Democratic candidates has not dropped below 94 percent as far back since at least 1989 (as far back as our records take us). In 2012, liberal candidates received $4.77 million compared to only $146,000 for conservatives.

Undoubtedly, when such large financial contributions flow in one direction—that is, the Democratic Party—some governors from this party responded by delaying implementation of the teacher evaluation component in RttT. Even though they committed to have this requirement in place by 2015, a degree of backtracking is evident.

On the other side of the political spectrum, some conservative elements within the Republican Party are attempting to discredit Common Core by claiming that the initiative is an example of federal overreach (a claim that this book discredits). Opposition evident from both ends of the political spectrum is a concern because political solutions to problems, even when they are unrelated, are too frequently resolved by endless delays, which eventually can scuttle the initiative.

OVERCOMING EARLY RESISTANCE AND CHANGE IN FOCUS

Fully implementing Common Core within all states of the original participants is experiencing some opposition. For example, Crouch (2015) reports, "Missouri public school children spent untold hours this spring prepping for a new computer-based standardized test. It required written essays, details to back up answers, and raised concerns that such a drastic change could overstress students and lead to lackluster results." This report begs the question whether "lackluster results" would occur because of change or use of higher quality tests?

After the legislature banned the tests, "work groups formed to recommend alternative standards have struggled with low attendance and, at times, dysfunction." Crouch reports on Representative Kurt Bahr's rationale for leading this charge:

> "My crusade against Common Core was never against the standards per se," Bahr said. "For me it was more of a state sovereignty issue. We lost state control of education. It was 'whose' standards they were, not 'what' standards they were." Bahr said he disliked the federal government's involvement in promoting the Common Core and the assessments. He wants learning standards to be set by Missourians, not by educators in other states. But he also disliked the computer-based as-

sessments that Smarter Balanced developed. He said that too many
poor districts didn't have the right technology in place, and that staring
at a computer screen for that long could lead to eye strain for students.

This book has already established that a de facto common core is in place
because states are tested using NAEP as well as international assessments—that is, TIMSS and PISA. A benefit in belonging to a consortium
of states pursuing higher standards is that the power of the group has the
capacity to drag along members experiencing internal resistance.

In a similar vein, Felton (2015) reports that two states—Indiana and
South Carolina—repealed the standards prior to 2015 but are reworking
the standards in a fashion similar to Common Core. These states can then
say to their constituents that they are no longer part of the Common Core
movement. In the 2014–2015 legislative sessions, nineteen states had bills
introduced to repeal Common Core, but these met with no success. Even
in what are considered very red states, such as Mississippi, Arizona, and
the Dakotas, no bills made it to the governors' desks. Felton further reports:

> "If you follow Twitter, watch Fox News or listen to [Republican presi-
> dential] candidates, you would think this is so unpopular that most
> states have dropped it," said Michael Petrilli, the president of the
> Thomas B. Fordham Institute, a conservative-leaning think tank that
> advocates for the standards. "But we've only lost one state, Oklahoma,
> and we have very red states still moving ahead with the Common
> Core."

This report goes on to explain that Republican opposition to the standards is withering in the face of opposition by the business community.
*Standards are what business really cares about, and funding support from busi-
ness is what the Republican Party cares about.*

Since repealing the standards is losing momentum, Felton reports that
the new target is the tests aligned with the standards. Quoting a university
researcher, Felton reports that the opposition to Common Core has
"moved away from just looking at the standards, which is nebulous to
people. The debate is moving away from less tangible standards to tangible assessments, accountability."

In this aspect of Common Core, common sense is flagging. At last
count, according to the Education Week website, as of February 20, 2015,
twenty-eight states plus the District of Columbia were planning to use
either the common assessments developed by the PARCC or Smarter

Balanced assessment consortia. In the early days of the Common Core, most states were expected to go with one or the other of those state coalitions. Now twenty-one states, including New York, Florida, Tennessee, and North Carolina, are going their own way.

The tragedy unfolding in these twenty-one states is that they are adopting the same scenario evident with NCLB (reported in figure 2.1), where states gamed the system by lowering the difficulty of their tests. Gewertz and Ujifusa (2014) write in *Education Week*:

> James W. Pellegrino, a distinguished professor of education at the University of Illinois-Chicago who serves on the technical-advisory committees of both testing consortia, said the trend "moves us back closer to where we were under No Child Left Behind." That federal law, though it sought to spur student achievement, left each state free to set its definition of "proficient" as low as it liked, he noted. . . . "With many different tests measuring students' learning," Mr. Pellegrino said, "the country loses the ability to reach a shared, rigorous definition of mastery or college readiness."

Abandoning common assessments, despite their governor's written commitment, provides these states with the wriggle room necessary to escape accountability and, coincidentally, negate fairness to their students. Herein is a classic example of why public skepticism regarding politicians is so high and trust in their decisions is so low. When the focus is primarily related to accountability, political commitment and follow-through wavers.

These states now risk losing their allotment of federal funding because they are abandoning the precondition of using common assessments. At the same time, some governors are faced with choosing qualified compliance by using common assessments but abandoning the minimum 95 percent participation rate from the NCLB. This wrinkle, too, can risk funding as well as hinder accountability.

The significance of Pellegrino's statement cannot be overlooked. The media must adopt a more aggressive position in revealing how parents and the public around the country are being duped. While administrators and their political masters are aware of the lack of transparency regarding the low standards employed in developing state tests, this fact is not understood in the place where this really matters: the court of public opinion.

On July 13, 2015, the Education Commission of the States, e-clips revealed a report on the 2013 NAEP results by stating that "when it comes to state standards, proficiency is still in the eye of the beholder." This new report, by the National Center for Education Statistics, compares each state's performance on state tests with their performance on the 2013 National Assessment of Educational Performance—or NAEP. New analysis from this national assessment shows differences in how states define "proficiency." For example, fourth-grade "proficient" reading standards in 28 states would be considered "below basic" under NAEP's benchmarks.

This report provides state scores on what is considered the gold standard for measuring performance in math and reading for grades 4 and 8. Comparing academic performance between states is difficult because many states have their own tests—aligned to their own standards. This inconsistency is one of the problems the Common Core is aimed at fixing. The data in this new 2013 report occurred before the new tests aligned with the Common Core were rolled out in many states. The report says:

> Comparing state tests to the NAEP helps to contextualize performance between states—apples to apples. Since 2003, this comparison has exposed huge differences in what states consider proficient, or at-grade-level and what NAEP defines as proficient.
>
> "Good assessments that are aligned well with good standards are very important," says Patte Barth, the director of the Center for Public Education, a policy arm of the National School Boards Association. "It gives everybody a good idea of what an eighth-grade student should know." NAEP breaks scores down into three levels: below basic, basic and proficient. The scores required for those achievement levels vary for different grades and for different subjects. To be proficient in math, for example, a fourth-grade student would need to score at least a 249 on NAEP's 500-point scale. A score below 214, is considered below basic and scores in between are basic.

Summarizing the results on the four tests, we find that:

- Alabama, Georgia, and Idaho score below basic on all four tests.
- New York is the only state scoring proficient on all four tests.
- Texas, Utah, Vermont, Virginia, Washington, West Virginia, and Wisconsin score proficient in mathematics for both grades and basic in reading for both grades.

- Massachusetts scores proficient in grade 4 math and at basic in the other three tests. North Carolina has a similar pattern except their proficiency is in grade 8 reading.
- For the fifty states on the four tests, proficiency scores occur twenty times (10 percent), whereas below basic scores occur on fifty-three occasions (26.5 percent).

Michael Cohen, president of Achieve, a nonprofit education research group, has said, "If we want students to graduate with the skills and knowledge expected by postsecondary education and employers, states must make sure that 'proficient' means that students are well prepared. Many states need to do a better job leveling with students and their parents."

Herein lies the crux of the problem: states are not leveling! Politicians and their administrators do not regard transparency on these matters as being in their best interests. Therefore special interests are able to capitalize on the public's ignorance when they make negative remarks about Common Core and common assessment.

Several states are grappling with assessment issues. Hammond (2015) reports that Oregon's Governor Brown may receive proposed legislation emanating from a House Bill receiving overwhelming support. Hammond reports:

> Backers [of the bill] want schools to inform Oregon parents twice a year of their rights to exempt children from state reading and math tests for any reason. Supporters also want schools where a lot of students go untested to be protected from the normal consequence of having the school's performance rating downgraded a notch or two.
>
> But Obama administration officials say testing all students *promotes civil rights*. Schools need to give an honest accounting of how well they prepare students of all backgrounds to meet state academic benchmarks, they argue, and incomplete testing blurs those determinations.

Oregon's governor may veto the bill because of financial pressure, which is a lever employed by the federal government to "stay the course." Hopefully this governor will affirm her state's commitment, not because of a financial penalty, but because of the educational benefit Oregon's students receive from Common Core and common assessment.

As Hammond (2015) reported a few weeks later:

> Gov. Kate Brown announced Tuesday that on Monday she signed a bill making it easier for parents to opt their children out of taking state

standardized tests. But she said educators and state officials should convince parents not to do so. . . . Brown said she wants Oregon educators to make the case to parents that taking part in state tests is valuable so that they will opt for their children to keep taking the exams. . . .

"Under HB 2655, the state is responsible to ensure parents are aware of the purpose and value of assessments and receive notice from their local school districts about their rights and obligations," she continued. "Educators must engage with parents about the value of assessment and the potential consequences if parents opt out and student participation diminishes."

In essence, the governor is hopeful that educators, fearful of having common assessments become part of their evaluation and subsequently influencing their pay, will assume a role in convincing parents that their child should participate in the testing program. Politicians are looking to find a way through the morass by transferring their leadership responsibilities to the rank and file.

With a similar situation, Ronayne (2015) reports on a decision by New Hampshire's governor Hassan to veto legislation that would have allowed parents to opt their students out of statewide, Common Core–aligned tests without consequences for the students or school districts.

In her veto message, Hassan said the bill could jeopardize federal funding and would send a message that New Hampshire doesn't value high standards. The statewide chamber of commerce sent Hassan a letter urging her to veto the bill.

"These tests provide the only statewide snapshot as to how our public schools are performing, serving as an additional measure to inform us about how well students are being educated," Hassan said. As a matter of interest, Republican Rep. JR Hoell, the bill's prime sponsor, said Hassan's veto shows that she favors heavy federal regulations in education. Hoell does not support the Common Core education standards that New Hampshire's tests are based on. "She is not interested in standing up for the parents' rights, nor what is best for children," Hoell said.

This report from New Hampshire demonstrates the usual political overtones evident in American politics. A Democratic governor is supporting the Democratic president. Republicans control the legislature, presenting a populist viewpoint of a vocal group that may or may not constitute a majority; however, loud voices receive more support than silent ones.

The political conflict features another voice (i.e., Chamber of Commerce), which understands the deeper issue and provides a politically aligned governor with public support to withstand the opposition.

In another Democratic state involved in political ping-pong, Delaware legislators in the House grappled with a controversial bill to allow parents to opt out of the state standardized test (Albright 2015). When the House originally signed off on the bill, it only allowed parents to opt out of the Smarter Balanced Assessment, the tough new state-wide standardized test. Amendments were added that extended the testing to include district tests and a change to allow high school juniors to make a choice about taking the test.

Political wrangling ensued culminating with the removal of students being allowed to opt-out based on the argument that it is not appropriate to allow minors to opt themselves out, especially if it's against the wishes of their own parents. Should this bill pass the Senate, Governor Markell, who opposes the bill, will have a choice to veto it, knowing that large margins of support for the bill in both houses suggest that lawmakers could overturn a veto.

Albright concludes the report with significant observations:

> Though some parents already pulled their kids out of the state's new Smarter Balanced Assessment, the Department of Education has said state law requires students take the test unless there are rare exceptions. Groups like the state Parent Teacher Association say that has led some districts to attempt to pressure parents away from opting out. The PTA said [the new] bill would prevent that. The PTA and other parent and teacher groups argued the Smarter Balanced test places too much stress on kids and takes away valuable class time without giving them any useful information. They said Delaware is relying too much on test scores to judge teachers and schools. Markell and his Department of Education strongly opposed the bill, saying the scores from Smarter Balanced will be essential to making smart education policy. The administration has enlisted the support of business leaders, who want to see accountability in schools, and civil rights groups, who say tests are an important way to make sure at-risk students aren't being left behind.

Teachers hold considerable sway over parents because of their close connections. When they say that these tests "take away valuable class time without giving them any useful information," and that "Delaware is relying too much on test scores to judge teachers and schools," their intention is to obfuscate the public, thereby negating efforts to increase accountability in the school system.

When the bill finally reached the governor's desk, Markell vetoed it; as a result, lawmakers and parent groups who supported the bill are furious and demanding the General Assembly override the action when it returns in January 2016, which would require a three-fifths majority in both chambers. According to Albright (2015), Markell's comment regarding his first veto of an education-related bill stated that the legislation

> would undermine the only objective tool we have to understand whether our children are learning and our schools are improving. It has the potential to marginalize our highest need students, threaten tens of millions of dollars of federal funding and undermine our state's economic competitiveness—all without adequately addressing the issues that motivated many to support the legislation.

Clearly this governor is pursuing a course of action that facilitates higher levels of fairness for students in Delaware. Placing students on the pinnacle of education policy requires courage, which he demonstrated as an original signatory of Common Core and which he is pursuing in common assessment. *Enlisting the support of the business community and minority groups can be strengthened if he can also demonstrate transparency in making the data available regarding the inconsistencies evident in how teachers assess student work.*

COMMON ASSESSMENTS HAVE SIGNIFICANT VALUE

Teachers also attempt to deflect the valuable information gleaned from high-quality testing such as is evident in the Smarter Balance tests used in Delaware. They claim that these tests "take away valuable class time without giving them any useful information." This claim is so contrary to what some researchers say. For example, Michael Fullan (2005) states:

> A by-product of external accountability, assessment *for* learning refers to "any assessment for which the first priority is to serve the purpose of promoting students' learning." Even using external tests as the criterion, Black et al. documented improvements in the results of most teachers, which, "if replicated across the whole school . . . would raise the performance of a school at the 25th percentile of achievement nationally into the upper half."

Douglas Reeves (2000) describes the value of common assessments using his research:

> I note that all schools with gains of more than 20 per cent in student achievement also happen to employ common assessments, extensive nonfiction writing, and collaborative scoring by the faculty, then I can begin to draw inferences that common assessments, nonfiction writing, and collaborative scoring are at the very least associated with improved student performance.

Reeves recognizes that the method most used by teachers when they undertake the only scoring for their students' work is actually poor practice. Inconsistency occurs when teachers allow their biases to influence their marking, whereas defending their marks with colleagues reviewing the same assignments improves consistency. Richard Stiggins, another assessment guru, reminds educators:

> There has been a misguided understanding about assessment *for* learning and assessment *of* learning. . . . The perception that assessment *of* learning is less valued or unacceptable practice has been used to marginalize external testing programs. Stiggins warns that teachers should not fall prey to pitting one kind of assessment against the other. Both assessments are important and should be used. (Webber et al. 2009)

These expert opinions are valuable in the ongoing debate regarding common assessments, and their contributions are reinforced by a 2009 national report in the United Kingdom. This report underscores the value of common assessment:

> An over-riding principle of a national assessment system is to make sure that the standards against which students are assessed are held at a consistent level over time; the maxim being "if you want to measure change don't change the measure." This is vital for international and intra-national comparisons. . . . Independently measuring pupils against national standards remains, in our view, the best way of providing objective information on the performance of each pupil and each school.

Delaware's Governor Markell, a strong supporter of Common Core from the outset, fortified his position by enlisting support of the business community and civil rights groups. Supporting fairness to students, who have no official representation and are without voting privileges, over the protectionist actions of teachers, who can summon an army of dissenting voices and have power in the voting booth, is placing this governor on the proverbial "horns of a dilemma."

New York also grapples with the teacher pay component in this matter of using student test scores for their process to evaluate teachers. Decker (2015) reports:

> The approved regulations allow school districts to create plans that give state tests and locally selected tests equal weight in a teacher's final rating. The state had proposed offering the "50-50" option only for districts considered to have high-quality local assessments available. The Regents extended that option to all districts in response to concerns that the state's tests would otherwise factor too heavily into evaluations.

Their decision introduces a compromise involving common assessment equaling a teacher's classroom test. In other words, a poor outcome on the common assessment can be overturned by the teacher preparing a test that likely does not undergo the scrutiny associated with developing valid and reliable tests. Teacher-made tests remove elements of consistency and may result in inflated grades because of easier tests. Chapter 6 already indicates the absurdities of this compromise, especially since the state backed away from limiting this practice to districts with a reputation for developing quality tests.

Identifying the marker is an additional aspect that potentially makes this compromise inappropriate. Teachers marking their own students' tests will feel a bias for giving test responses some degree of "benefit of the doubt" because of implications these tests have on their evaluation and pay. At the very least, teachers must not mark their own students' tests.

For readers who are attracted to conspiracy thinking, the dilemma of attaching student achievement data to educator evaluations and then pay provides fodder for a potential conspiracy. What is fair for the goose is fair for the gander, and if the practitioners of education receive reward and compensation for student success, should those who administer and make policy also be recognized? In other words, should teachers experience higher forms of accountability than their leaders?

A MORAL PRINCIPLE IN ACCOUNTABILITY

Reeves (2002) prescribes an accountability moral principle as having "no child in any school more accountable than the adults in the system. Similarly, is a moral principle of leadership that no teacher or staff member will be more accountable than the leaders in the [school] system." State politicians are responsible for educational outcomes and assume the highest level of leadership for the education system. To what extent are they cognizant of this moral principle?

They may not fully understand their place in the hierarchical structure for education, which is but one of the departments in state governance. If it is now becoming apparent within some political offices that there is a two-way street, anxiety within politicians may also be evident. That is, leadership in the classroom flows down from the State House, the school district office, and the school office. Accountability based on measures of student success can follow the same path from the classroom up to the school office, the school district office, and the State House.

Reeves's moral principle claims that no teacher will be held more accountable than the leadership. When a teacher's evaluation incorporates student outcomes, thereby impacting their pay, there should be an expectation that all levels of leadership are similarly recognized and rewarded. Everyone in the education system is consumed with fairness to students within their sphere of influence.

With some politicians now struggling over this issue of locating students to the top of the pyramid or pinnacle, are they already understanding how accountability may embrace them? On the one hand, people readily understand that politicians base their decisions on votes, which, in this context, come from teachers. On the other hand, people inclined toward conspiracy thinking may believe that politicians who express negativity regarding making the education system fairer for students are fearful of being held to the same principles of accountability. For this group, cheering on the accountability movement is a non-starter.

HIGHER EDUCATION JOINS THE FRAY

While aspects of Common Core are progressing as planned through most of the states where governors requested it, this chapter identifies opposition that politicians are dealing with beyond the political maneuvering identified in chapter 4, which demonstrated that politicians are gaming for votes by using specious arguments to capture voters' attention. This chapter is more about power and control where teachers want to subvert a process that replaces them atop the pyramid.

Higher education can play an important role in encouraging politicians to hold the course. An online release dated July 7, 2015, from Higher Ed for Higher Standards, National Association of System Heads (NASH), and State Higher Education Executive Officers Association (SHEEO), issued a *joint statement demonstrating their support for Common Core.* The concise nature of their common sense makes it worthy to incorporate their entire document in this book.

Ensuring That Proficient Means Prepared: Higher Education's Commitment
to College- and Career-Ready Standards and Assessments

July 7, 2015

States have made great strides over the past several years in implementing more challenging K–12 standards designed to prepare students for success in college and careers. As leaders in the higher education community, we applaud that work, as it holds tremendous potential for increasing the number of students who arrive in our colleges and in businesses prepared for success. The need for higher standards is clear. Each year, about 50 percent of first-year students at two-year colleges and 20 percent of those entering four-year universities require basic developmental courses before they can begin credit-bearing coursework. This lack of preparedness costs students and taxpayers billions of dollars each year. It stagnates our educational system and exacerbates the business community's problem of filling jobs. On the international stage, our students trail as well. On the latest Programme for International Student Assessment (PISA) taken by high school students around the world, U.S. students rank 36th in math, 28th in science, and 24th in reading. And according to a recent study by the Educational Testing Service, young adults in the United States (ages 16–34) rank at or near the bottom on international comparisons of problem solving, numeracy, and literacy skills.

This preparation gap is large and persistent. It puts our students at risk, and it threatens the health of our economy. Setting higher expectations for student learning is absolutely necessary if we are to close these gaps that now leave our young people at such a competitive disadvantage. This summer and fall will mark a critical milestone in states' efforts to raise educational standards: The results of new K–12 student assessments will be released in states across the country. These new assessments represent a major step forward for students, as well as for colleges and employers. For the first time, scores on high school assessments will have a meaningful connection to college and career success: Meeting standards will mean that students are prepared for successful transition into credit bearing college coursework and training opportunities. Because the assessments have been purposefully pegged to a higher standard than previous state tests—a college- and career-ready standard—we expect the initial scores to be lower than what students, families and educators are used to. This should not be cause for alarm nor an indictment of our K–12 educators. The tests are simply providing a more accurate assessment of our students' readiness for the demands of postsecondary life, the need for which is validated by our own remediation numbers and employer surveys. An honest assessment of students' readiness for postsecondary pursuits taken prior to high school graduation will give educators in every state a starting point to develop pathways and supports to help more students make a successful transition.

We urge our states to remain committed to high standards. We must not back down if initial results are low. The new standards and assessments are anchored in what it takes to succeed in college and careers. We owe it to our students to maintain these higher expectations and do what it takes to help them succeed. We are committed to working closely with our K–12 colleagues to ensure that the standards and assessments are used to support student success. The new assessments provide critical information that will allow us to identify and address skills gaps while students are still in high school, so they arrive at our institutions and work places better prepared. We must harness these new measures to provide targeted supports and opportunities for acceleration for our high school students, such as 12th grade bridge courses, dual enrollment opportunities, and course offerings aligned to career pathways. We must also be prepared to change practices in our higher education institutions to provide for smoother transitions for students who meet the new standards. This will include adapting our placement policies to take the new standards and assessments into account and examining freshman gateway courses to ensure they are part of clear pathways that build from the new K–12 standards and lead to meaningful degrees and credentials. We also have a responsibility to prepare new teachers and assist veteran teachers in the delivery of high-quality instruction supporting these higher standards. We have a once-in-a-generation opportunity to close the preparation gap by remaining committed to high expectations and doubling down on policies and programs to support student success. We must press ahead with this important work.

With this statement, higher education plants its flag of support for Common Core and the assessment program associated with it. The most significant comment is this: "Each year, about 50 percent of first-year students at two-year colleges and 20 percent of those entering four-year universities require basic developmental courses before they can begin credit-bearing coursework." In other words, standards currently in the school system are far below what are required for success in post-secondary and business.

The second critical point reminds the public that test results may be lower than expected. "The tests are simply providing a more accurate assessment of our students' readiness for the demands of postsecondary life, the need for which is validated by our own remediation numbers and employer surveys," the release says. In other words, the common assessment approach will counter much of the grade inflation prevalent in the school system.

The political elements across the country now "have a *once-in-a-generation opportunity* to close the preparation gap by remaining committed." They must now say, "If it is to be, it is up to we." There is a saying that the word "if" is the biggest word in the English language because it portends a need to overcome some challenging circumstances. Change is always difficult, and implementing Common Core successfully requires steadfast commitment from those with political power.

The key points made in this chapter are as follows:

- Early support for Common Core by educators and ambivalence from the media and the public changed after the 2012 American elections to the extent that tensions are building for the 2016 elections.
- Teachers' support for unions is flagging; however, concern over pay-for-performance provides unions with opportunity to reenergize support.
- Political opposition within most states is insufficient to counter the business community's support.
- Opposition to common assessment now replaces opposition to Common Core.

- Abandoning common assessments provides states with the wriggle room necessary to escape accountability and, coincidentally, negate fairness to their students.
- Common assessments are valuable for classroom teaching.
- A moral principle is that no student be held to a higher degree of accountability than their teacher, and no teacher should be more accountable than their leadership.
- Higher education organizations strongly endorse Common Core and common assessment.

Conclusion

American education is preoccupied with one of its most transformative initiatives in this generation, christened with the confusing title of "Common Core." These standards reflect an understanding among American politicians that the highest-performing countries create high, consistent expectations for student learning. Wide discrepancies in state standards are seen currently as one of the reasons why the United States is not as competitive as it once was.

Until now, the word "core" was not an educational term, and it is creating confusion within the general population, who have conjured up their own understandings of the term. Many opposing this initiative assume that the term is synonymous with "curriculum" and that what has always been a local decision (at least within each state) is now going to be nationalized. When the public is advised that Common Core actually refers to common standards, support increases to a reasonable majority.

Confusion is also apparent with respect to the origin of this initiative, which is increasing its politicization because of possible ties to a specific political party. As a matter of record, Common Core emerged at the request of forty-five governors who wanted to increase standards of learning across their states. Confusion regarding this initiative is contributing to its status as a political issue in the 2016 elections, which may (or may not) bring greater clarity and unity regarding how it should proceed.

In the early stages of implementation, the media was somewhat indifferent until special interests became more vocal. Controversy is an important driver for the media because they can profit when opposing perspectives are displayed in the public arena. Myths regarding Common Core make this a controversial issue, which provides a means for garnering support from certain candidates. Questions regarding the appropriate level of government involvement for issues such as Common Core are feeding this controversy.

Not only is Common Core conflicted by terminology and mandate, but it also deals with a fundamental human value: trust. Therefore, this book deals extensively with trust or, rather, the lack of it. Most states compromised trust when they tested student achievement in No Child Left Behind. Manipulating test difficulty to qualify for improvement awards in NCLB is a critical point for readers. The public is generally unaware that manipulating test difficulty is relatively easy and that student achievement can be portrayed as better than it really is. *Grade inflation is an educational disease constantly in search of an antidote.*

Trust, however, is equally troublesome in the classroom when teachers allow biases to influence their assessments of student achievement. The phrase "shooting the messenger" is understood especially well within the school system. *Standardized testing, which provides hard data on performance, continues to be the focus of concerted attacks by teachers and their unions because their results allow comparability.* Now that their success in achieving significant student outcomes is under a microscope, their thrust is to *kill this unwanted messenger.* If they succeed, the unfortunate result is that a significant portion of students will continue to be treated unfairly.

In the political arena we witness many politicians waffling from pursuing the goal of fairness for students to a less honorable pursuit of pandering for votes. It is disappointing when politicians "sign on" as equal participants in a program and then renege when faced with some opposition from special interests, due mostly to confusion over terminology. It is unconscionable when politicians permit a reduction in standards so that students' academic performance is inflated.

It is also distressing to learn how *teachers' marks of student learning lack consistency and tend toward significant grade inflation.* Not only does the school system suffer from having low standards within the teaching profession, but these practitioners also have low expectations of too many students. As professionals, teachers need to acknowledge that their humanness leads to unfairness for students rather than display defensive reactions, either as individuals or as part of an organized workforce such as a union.

Common Core is necessary for parents to feel certain that their children are receiving the quality of education they deserve and require. In our global village, taxpayers need assurance that their elected representatives are not hiding their failed leadership in providing high-quality education by dumbing down standards. Negative leadership occurs when our political leadership confuses the public into thinking that homemade standards are superior when, in fact, they are used to wiggle out of accountability when results are inferior to other regions.

There is a necessity to link common assessment with Common Core so that Americans can determine where are the *islands of excellence* within their school, community, state, or nation. The public benefits when a common form of measurement is available to demonstrate whether leadership is positive or negative, and parents benefit from knowing whether their child's teacher is providing effective service.

Common assessment of student achievement relative to common standards provides the school system with a more meaningful way to recognize and reward educators. The profession will be the beneficiary of greater status when educators receive remuneration and reward based on their contribution to their central responsibility: student learning. *When something is valued, we assign greater accountability to it.* It is a sure signal that teachers and the school system are valued and respected when accountability ensures that teachers' pay is influenced by student outcomes.

Linking Common Core, common assessment and teachers' pay provides the framework necessary for transforming America's education system, so that there will not be a future report titled *A Nation at Risk II*. Hollywood entices us with sequels; however, there must not be any repeat of the conclusion for American's education system that "if an unfriendly foreign power had attempted to impose on America the mediocre educational performance that exists today, we might well have viewed it as an act of war."

Overcoming public apathy and correcting misinformation concerning Common Core and its related components articulated in this book requires full transparency. The media relishes using data in news stories, as witnessed by their reports on medical studies. It is common to see releases repeating studies about the effects on people's lives from taking, or not taking, certain drugs. For example, is an aspirin a day truly helpful?

Admittedly, using data in areas such as health poses a limited threat for the media. Much of their reporting in this aspect of our society is impersonal. That is, reporting on health issues usually does not impugn an identified body of people; rather, it is a company's product that is the focus. Only periodically is the public alerted about malpractice within the health profession. Reports about poor practice by individuals are more likely because the reporting agency is less likely to face retribution from the entire group when the focus is on an individual.

The situation in education is radically different. "Wellness" in each learner can be determined, as can the degree of improvement in that wellness. Second opinions are constantly available, regardless of whether these come from the teacher in the subsequent year or from standardized assessments. Health issues at any point in time deal with subgroups of the population; however, education is universal and involves almost everyone.

Data from the school system eventually is pointed at people, teachers, and administrators. Their representatives—for example, unions—are powerful and represent a significant political force in our society because teachers are one of the largest worker groups in the country. Politicians believe that workers in education are instrumental in winning political power. Media understand that reporting negative results in education can endanger their financial bottom line. Parents, who seldom have the luxury of relocating their child to a different situation, believe that complaining about services provided to their child will come back to haunt that child.

In this environment, education administrators are key players. They have access to all of the data referenced in this book and much more. Their positions provide an obvious platform to display information to their political masters and the public, but they must possess the courage to bring the information forward. In other words, they can easily be a screen or filter blocking information from getting into the public arena.

When administrators perceive that teachers are at the top of the educational pyramid in their district because their political masters are too aligned with teachers, they will likely be hesitant in their commitment to transparency. An ongoing question in administrators' minds is whether their performance evaluations will be based more on student outcomes or on popularity with staff. The reality of human nature may influence a well-intentioned administrator to be less forthcoming with information when the latter condition prevails.

Which group occupies the pinnacle in education is critical. The issues identified in this book prevail when students are not at the top. When they are, Common Core will be implemented, and it will be linked with common assessment; these results will inform staff evaluations, which will impact pay. Where these factors are combined, students will experience their most fair learning situation.

Important in this stage of U.S. history is the eventual outcome of the 2016 presidential election and this future leader's vision for education. Will the new president's vision see students rather than workers at the top of education's pinnacle? Increasing fairness to the nation's children requires supporting Common Core linked with common assessment, with outcomes from these assessments contributing to teachers' evaluations, which, in turn, have a bearing on teachers' pay.

RECOMMENDATIONS

This book's central message communicates the first and foremost need for politicians to hold the course of implementing Common Core and linking this component with common assessment. Accompanying this commitment is a requirement to ensure that teacher evaluations contain, where applicable, a component based on their students' improvement in scores on these common assessments, and that these evaluations influence how these teachers are paid.

Second, we must hold educators and schools to the same level of accountability that they hold students, who are evaluated across many subjects and on multiple components within a subject, involving multiple ratings such as letter grades or percentages. Teacher and principal evaluations should contain rating scales with multiple levels and multiple criteria within their evaluations.

Third, fairness to students necessitates a reduction in grade inflation by requiring teachers to partner with another teacher for marking subjective assignments. The partnering teacher should not be familiar with the students.

Fourth, we must increase the integrity of teachers' assessments of student progress by providing parents with an annual summary in language arts and mathematics indicating whether the learner's achievement is "at," "above," or "below" their grade placement.

References

Adler, J. "Debate: Are Teachers' Unions the Problem—or the Answer?" *Newsweek*, March 18, 2010.

Albright, M. "Delaware House Passes Opt-Out Bill After See-Saw Drama." *News Journal*, June 24, 2015.

Albright, M. "Markell Vetoes Delaware Testing Opt-Out Bill." *News Journal*, July 16, 2015.

Anderson, J. "Curious Grade for Teachers: Nearly All Pass." *New York Times*, March 30, 2013.

Babcock, P. "Real Costs of Nominal Grade Inflation? New Evidence from Student Course Evaluations." *Economic Inquiry* 48, no. 4 (October 2010).

Bamesberger, Michael. "Nebraska's Master's Degree Bonuses for Teachers May Need Refiguring." *Daily Nebraskan*, February 3, 2011.

Bevan, Y., Brighouse, T., Mills, G., Rose, J., and Smith, M. *Report of the Expert Group on Assessment*. 2009. http://publications.education.gov.uk/eOrderingDownload/Expert-Group-Report.pdf.

Bidwell, A. "Public School Teachers Accuse Duncan of Undermining Education." *U.S. News and World Report*, July 14, 2014.

Bidwell, A. "Duncan Relaxes Testing Push, But Teachers Want More." *U.S. News and World Report*, August 21, 2014.

Bishop, J. H. *High School Exit Examinations: When Do Learning Effects Generalize?* Cornell University, 2005.

Black, Conrad. "Public-Sector Unions Are a Blight on Our Society." *National Post*, May 4, 2013.

Borzelleca, D. "The Male-Female Ratio in College." *Forbes*, February 16, 2012.

Brown, L. *Common Core Political Fight Heats Up*. CNBC, March 31, 2015.

Buddin, R., and Zamarro, G. "Teacher Qualifications and Student Achievement in Urban Elementary Schools." *Journal of Urban Economics* 66, no. 2 (September 2009).

Bushway, A., and Nash, W. R. "School Cheating Behaviour." *Review of Educational Research* 47, no. 4 (1977): 623–632.

Camera, L. "Polls Capture Public's Sour View of Common Core." *Education Week*, March 15, 2015.

Cameron, J., and Pierce, D. *Rewards and Intrinsic Motivation: Resolving the Controversy*. Alberta: University of Alberta Press, 2002.

Cote, J. "Making the Grade." *Queen's Journal*, September 19, 2009.

Crouch, E. "Missouri Legislature Throws Common Core Test Out the Window." *St. Louis Post-Dispatch*, June 4, 2015.

Cunningham, W. G., and Owens, R. C. "Social Promotion: Problem or Solution?" *NASSP Bulletin* 60, no. 402 (October 1976): 25–29.

Davis, J., and Smith, T. *General Social Surveys, 1972–1994*. Chicago: NORC, 1994.

Davis, S. F., Drinan, P. F., and Gallant, T. B. *Cheating in School.* West Sussex, UK: Wiley-Blackwell, 2009.

Decker, G. "New Evaluation Rules Win Final Approval, with Some Regents Still Opposed." *Chalkbeat,* June 16, 2015.

Decoo, W. *Crisis on Campus: Confronting Academic Misconduct.* Cambridge, MA: MIT Press, 2002.

Dillon, E., and Rotherham, A. "States' Evidence: What It Means to Make 'Adequate Yearly Progress' Under NCLB." Education Sector, July 24, 2007.

Dobbins, H., and Bentsen, L. "A Hidden Cost of Common Core: Teacher Accountability." National Center for Policy Analysis, November 12, 2014.

Dueck, J. *Being Fair With Kids.* New York: Rowman & Littlefield, 2013.

Editorial Projects in Education Research Center. "Issues A–Z: Social Promotion." *Education Week,* August 4, 2004. http://www.edweek.org/ew/issues/social-promotion/.

Farkas, S., Johnson, J., and Duffett, A. *Stand By Me: What Teachers Really Think About Unions, Merit Pay and Other Professional Matters.* Public Agenda (2003). www.publicagenda.org/files/stand_by_me.pdf.

Felton, E. "Opponents of Common Core Open New Fronts in Battle Against Standards After a Series of Defeats." *Hechinger Report,* March 5, 2015.

Fullan, M. *Leadership and Sustainability.* Thousand Oaks, CA: Sage, 2005.

Gewertz, C., and Ujifusa, A. "National Landscape Fragments as States Plan Common-Core Testing." *Education Week,* May 21, 2014.

Goe, L., and Stickler, L. M. "Teacher Quality and Student Achievement: Making the Most of Recent Research." *TQ and Policy Research Brief* (2008).

Goodwin, B. "Research Says / Grade Inflation: Killing with Kindness?" *Educational Leadership* 69, no. 3 (November 2011).

Greene, J. P. *Education Myths.* New York: Rowman & Littlefield, 2005.

Greene, J. P., and Winters, M. A. "Test-Based Promotion Proves Its Mettle." *National Review* (2011).

Grier, P. "Election Results 2012: Who Won It for Obama?" *Christian Science Monitor,* November 27, 2012.

Grissom, J., Nicholson-Crotty, S., and Harrington, J. "High-Stakes Choice: Achievement and Accountability in the Nation's Oldest Urban Voucher Program." *Educational Evaluation and Policy Analysis,* December 1, 2014: 437–456.

Guggino, P., and Brint, S. "Teachers Give No Child Left Behind Act Mixed Reviews." *UCRiverside Newsroom,* January 26, 2010.

Hammond, B. "Oregon Risks Losing $140 Million for Enabling Kids to Skip Common Core Tests, Feds Warn." *Oregonian,* June 9, 2015.

Hammond, B. "Kate Brown Signs Bill Making It Easier for Parents to Opt Students Out of State Tests—But Says They Shouldn't." *Oregonian,* June 23, 2015.

Hanushek, E. "How Teachers' Unions Use 'Common Core' to Undermine Reform." *Wall Street Journal,* June 30, 2014.

Harkness, K. "Amidst Conservative Backlash, House Pulls No Child Left Behind." *Daily Signal,* February 27, 2015.

Harlen, W. "A Systematic Review of the Evidence of the Impact on Students, Teachers and the Curriculum of the Process of Using Assessment by Teachers for Summative Purposes." *Research Evidence in Education Library.* London: EPPI-Centre, Social Science Research Unit, Institute of Education, University of London, 2004.

Harris, D. N., and Sass, T. R. "Teacher Training, Teacher Quality, and Student Achievement." National Center for Analysis of Longitudinal Data in Education Research (March 2008).

Hawke, P. "Report Card on Florida Schools Policy to End Social Promotion." ezinearticles.com, 2006.

Hughes-Jones, D., Alexander, C., Rudo, Z., Pan, D., and Vaden-Kiernan, M. *Teacher Resources and Student Achievement in High-Need Schools Research Report* (January 2006).

Jensen, B., and Reichl, J. *Better Teacher Appraisal and Feedback: Improving Performance.* Melbourne: Grattan Institute, 2011.

Karweit, N. L. *Grade Retention: Prevalence, Timing, and Effects (Report No. 33).* Baltimore: Johns Hopkins University, CRESPAR, 1999.

Klein, R. "Majority of Americans Would Probably Support the Common Core, If They Knew What It Was." *Huffington Post,* February 19, 2014.

Koedel, C. "Grade Inflation for Education Majors and Low Standards for Teachers." American Enterprise Institute (August 2011).

Laurie, L. *Grade Inflation Sets Up Students to Fail: Study.* Halifax, Nova Scotia: Atlantic Institute for Marketing, 2007.

Linn, R., Baker, E., and Betebenner, D. "Accountability Systems: Implications of Requirements of the No Child Left Behind Act of 2001." *Educational Researcher* 31, no. 6 (August–September 2002): 3–16.

Lorence, J. "Retention and Academic Achievement Research Revisited from a United States Perspective." *International Education Journal* 7 (2006): 731–777.

Loveless, T. *Common Core Political Fight Heats Up.* CNBC, March 31, 2015.

Lurie, S. "Why Doesn't the Constitution Guarantee the Right to Education?" *Atlantic,* October 16, 2013.

Mak, T. "Arne Duncan: Pay Great Teachers $150K." *Politico,* January 27, 2012.

McCabe, D., Trevino, L., and Butterfield, K. *Cheating in Academic Institutions: A Decade of Research.* Mahwah, NJ: Lawrence Erlbaum, 2001.

McCombs, J. S., Kirby, S. N., and Mariano, L. T. *Ending Social Promotion Without Leaving Children Behind: The Case of New York City.* Santa Monica, CA: RAND Corporation, 2009.

Mellon, E. "HISD Moves Ahead on Dismissal Policy." *Houston Chronicle,* January 14, 2010.

Merrefield, Clark. "States With the Smartest Kids." *Daily Beast,* January 23, 2011.

Newberger, E. *The Men They Will Become: The Nature and Nurture of the Male Character.* New York: Perseus, 1999.

Niels, G. "Top Reasons Why Students Cheat." About.com, January 17, 2014.

Peterson, P., Howell, W., and West, M. "Teachers' Unions Have a Popularity Problem." *Wall Street Journal,* June 4, 2012.

Petrilli, M. "Common Core Supporters Run Ads in Iowa." *Wall Street Journal,* March 4, 2015.

Phelps, R. *Kill the Messenger: The War on Standardized Testing.* New Brunswick, NJ: Transaction, 2003.

Reeder, S. *Why Are Failing Teachers Getting a Passing Grade?* An investigative report by Small Newspaper Group, 2005.

Reeves, D. *Accountability in Action: A Blueprint for Learning Organizations.* Denver, CO: Advanced Learning Centers, 2000.

Reeves, D. "Six Principles of Effective Accountability: Accountability-Based Reforms Should Lead to Better Teaching and Learning-Period." *Harvard Education Letter* 18, no. 2 (March/April 2002).

Ronayne, K. "Hassan Vetoes Bill Letting Students Opt Out of State Tests." *Concord Monitor*, June 13, 2015.

Roza, M., and Miller, R. "Issue Brief: Separation of Degrees." *Generation Progress*, July 21, 2009.

Ryan, J. *Student Plagiarism in an On-line World. ASEE Prism* (December 1998).

Scantelbury, K. "Gender Bias in Teaching." Education.com, December 23, 2009.

Schmidt, W. "The Common Core State Standards in Mathematics." *Huffington Post Education*, November 5, 2012.

Smarick, A. "Homeostasis and the End of Today's Era of Reform?" Thomas B. Fordham Institute, December 11, 2014.

Thomas, M. D., and Bainbridge, W. "Grade Inflation: The Current Fraud." *Effective School Research* (January 1997).

Thompson, C. L., and Cunningham, E. K. *Retention and Social Promotion*. New York: ERIC Clearinghouse on Urban Education, 2000.

Van Wijngaarden, W. "How to Reward True High School Academic Excellence." University Affairs, September 25, 2013.

Wall, C. *The Skewing of the Bell Curve: A Study of Grade Inflation in Oklahoma High Schools*. Biosurvey.ou.edu/oas/03/paper/wall.htm, 2003.

Warren, J. "Chicago Teachers Union Winning? What Rahm Emanuel Is Up Against?" *Daily Beast*, September 12, 2012.

Webber, C., Aitken, N., Lupart, J., and Scott, S. *The Alberta Student Assessment Study*. The Crown in Right of Alberta, 2009.

Weisberg, D., Sexton, S., Mulhern, J., and Keeling, D. *The Widget Effect*. The New Teacher Project, 2009.

Williams, A. "The New Math on Campus." *New York Times*, February 5, 2010.

Williamson, R. *What Gets Measured Gets Done: Are You Measuring What Really Matters?* Strategic Work Systems, Inc. Columbus, NC, 2006.

Wolfgang, B. "Common Core Retains Outspoken Supporters Despite Conservative Backlash." *Washington Times*, May 3, 2015.

Xiang, Y., Dahlin, M., Cronin, J., Theaker, R., and Durant, S. "Do High Performing Students Maintain Their Altitude?" *Performance Trends of Top Performing Students*. Thomas B. Fordham Institute, September 20, 2011.

Zwaagstra, M., and Clifton, R. "An 'F' for Social Promotion." *Frontier Backgrounder* (August 2009).

Index

Abell Foundation, 141

accountability: CCSS strengthening, 27, 130, 131, 194–195; Hanushek on, 138; as investment, 118; moral principle of, 102, 104, 106, 187, 197; under NCLB, 45–46, 47; Pawlenty for, 133–134; of school administrators, 107–110, 197; social promotion reducing, 2, 162; teachers opposing, 7, 32, 59; transparency for, 67, 113, 122, 145, 148–149, 158–159, 173, 179, 181, 184, 195, 196; trust bolstered by, 7, 44, 54, 131, 194–195, 197

Achieve: Cohen of, 181; educational polling of, 7

ACT. *See* American College Testing

Adequate Yearly Progress (AYP): Linn on objectives of, 46; of NCLB, 44

administrators, school: accountability of, 107–110, 197; assessment subjectivity of, 134–136, 196; assessment success for, 121–123, 196; classroom visits of, 103–104; funding as performance measure of, 49, 59, 110–113; performance assessment of, 107–110; politics of measuring, 109–110, 196; teacher assessments by, 104–106; on teaching to test, 124–125

AFT. *See* American Federation of Teachers

Albany *Times Union*, 148

Alberta: assessments standardized in, 69–71; dropout rate low in, 120; grade inflation in, 70–73, 117, 118; grade-level assessment in, 172; grades compared with Ontario, 69–71; non-academic assessment criteria in, 81–84; regional

disparities limiting, 72–73; teacher certification studies in, 143; teacher experience years and pay in, 143–144; as tops in PISA tests, 117

Albright, M., 183–184

American College Testing (ACT), 73–74

American Federation of Teachers (AFT): on CCSS, 150–151; against Duncan, 147; evidence-based measures opposed by, 138, 175; lean to Democratic Party, 176–177; McElroy of, 47; membership in, 41; Weingarten of, 147, 150

American Recovery and Reinvestment Act (2009) (ARRA): AYP targets of, 44; pilot assessment programs of, ix–x, 44, 52–54; Title I, Part A funding of, 44, 45–46

American School Board Journal, 98–99

American voters: accountability bolsters trust of, 7, 44, 54, 131, 194–195, 197; CCSS acceptance of, 7, 35; demographics changes in, 35; education failing expectations of, 4–5, 41; fewer children of, 38; grade inflation naivety of, 75, 193–194; media failing, 9–10, 195–196; as oblivious to CCSS, 6; as stupid to Gruber, 5–6

Anderson, J.: on low standards, 149, 150; on teacher dismissal, 149

anonymous marking: fairness from, 64, 93, 96–97, 98, 101, 197; study of, 63, 64, 65, 79, 93, 96–97, 98, 101–102

ARRA. *See* American Recovery and Reinvestment Act

assessments: administration subjectivity in, 134–136, 196; of administrator performance,